"With *Grace in Tension*, Claire McGarry gives us the G-I-F-T of spiritual empowerment to face life's conflicts, stress, and stumbles with a new perspective. Claire openly shares from her own challenges while accompanying us along a proactive path to prayerful transformation. Life is full of rough stuff these days. *Grace in Tension* frames a terrific method for letting God walk with us even when times are difficult. A powerful, proactive prescription!"

Lisa M. Hendey, author of *The Grace of Yes*

"In a time when so many people are experiencing tension, stress, anxiety, and fear in the face of the world's many challenges, Claire McGarry reminds us to rediscover the grace of God in our midst. Drawing on the powerful scriptural witness of the Gospel of Luke, McGarry invites us to see Mary and Martha as companions in our contemporary spiritual journeys. The reflections in this book provide readers with practical opportunities to renew our way of seeing the world and deepen our prayer lives by putting our faith into action."

Daniel P. Horan, OFM, Director of the Center for Spirituality at Saint Mary's College, Notre Dame, IN and author of *God is Not Fair and Other Reasons for Gratitude*

"Are you striving to be a Mary in a Martha world? I think we all know which woman we *should* be, but deep down we can all admit which one we really are. Claire McGarry's book, *Grace in Tension*, gave me new eyes to that passage in Luke, showed me how to unpack it deeper, rejoice in being both a Mary and a Martha and see the G-I-F-T of it all. Brava, Claire!"

Kathryn Whitaker, author of *Live Big, Love Bigger*

"For Catholic women who, like me, deeply identify with Martha in her worry and distraction, Claire McGarry's balanced discussion of how busy women can learn to sit at the feet of Jesus is both a challenge and a gift. Learn to find the grace amid your daily cares and burdens."

Barb Szyszkiewicz, editor at CatholicMom.com and author of *The Handy Little Guide to Prayer*

"Discover the gifts of grace and peace amid life's tensions. With a fresh approach to the story of Mary and Martha, Claire McGarry uses heartfelt language, humor, relatable stories, and practical advice that illuminate insights into Jesus' love. There are important life lessons for every reader to find."

Shanna Crowell, speaker, blogger, women's ministry leader, Centerpoint Community Church, Salem, NH

"Each chapter reads like a personal devotion, filled with relatable stories, questions, and a fresh-look exposition of Mary and Martha from the Gospels of Luke and John. Claire systematically unpacks the theme of moving toward grace amidst the tension of life's circumstances. *Grace In Tension* is an enjoyable reminder of Christ's gentle 'nudge' toward receiving and giving His grace in our lives."

Rev. Zachary Crowell, MDIV, pastor,
Centerpoint Community Church, Salem, NH

"Claire McGarry introduces a unique and masterful approach to contemplating the Scripture on Mary and Martha. She marvelously illuminates each aspect of these Bible verses, which opens the reader to experience a deeper awareness of faith and of themselves. *Grace in Tension* is incredibly healing, inspiring, and empowering!"

Allison Gingras creator of the
Stay Connected Journals for Catholic Women (OSV)

"If you have never thought of stress as a gift, pray this book. Claire seamlessly blends everyday holiness with its challenge of prayer and responsibility and the Scripture story of Mary and Martha. In so doing, Claire reminds us that 'Today is a gift. That's why it's called the Present' (Bill Keane via Eleanor Roosevelt)."

Sister Bridget Haase, OSU, author of
Thirty Days Praying the Imitation of Christ
(www.wisdomwonder.com)

"In *Grace in Tension*, Claire McGarry provides readers with a treasury of concise yet deeply spiritual reflections. With engaging anecdotes that have universal appeal, McGarry invites us to examine the intricacies of the relationship between Martha and Mary while showing us how all our relationships, including our relationship with Jesus, can be strengthened through God's grace."

Terence Hegarty, editor of the U.S. edition of *Living with Christ*

"Like McGarry, I am a Martha. So, the structure of her book flowed wonderfully for me as a devotional resource. I would recommend it to anyone struggling with 'doing' over 'being.' McGarry's G-I-F-T is a gift to help us Gauge, Invite, and Filter so to be spiritually Transformed."

Rev. Dr. Lawrence Jay, Ordained American Baptist Pastor
and Executive Director of Rolling Ridge Retreat and Conference
Center, a ministry of the New England United Methodist Church

"In spite of identifying herself as a 'Martha' who is always too busy to sit and listen, Claire McGarry definitely proves herself to be a 'Mary' for her readers. She truly listens to Jesus' messages in the Bible, and helps deliver his truths to us. This inspiring book is a must-read for both individual and group study."

Pastor Mary Lindberg, Chaplain, Columbia Lutheran Home

"In her book, *Grace in Tension*, McGarry offers us practical wisdom and a pragmatic approach for discerning the tensions that keep us from moving forward in faith. The G-I-F-T method of prayer brings Scripture alive, makes it more accessible, and more present in our daily struggles. A must read for anyone looking to conquer the tensions that undermine their emotional and spiritual growth!"

Paul O'Keeffe, OFM, MTS, LICSW

"Warning lights. Tug-of-war scarves. Currents. They all can be signs of tension — or signs that grace is at hand. Claire McGarry shares poignant, sometimes funny, stories from her own life as she cracks open Scripture on sisters Mary and Martha — and gently shows us the gifts with which God lavishes us when we trust."

Melanie Rigney, *Sisterhood of Saints* (www.rejoicebeglad.com)

"Our natural inclination is to push stress and tension away. But through her insightful and Spirit-guided reflections on Martha and Mary, Claire McGarry invites us to look more deeply into that tension to discover the gift of true peace that lies within. A game-changer for us all!"

Lindsay Schlegel, author of *Don't Forget to Say Thank You: And Other Parenting Lessons That Brought Me Closer to God*

Grace IN TENSION

Discover Peace with Martha and Mary

Claire McGarry

Our Sunday Visitor
Huntington, Indiana

Our Sunday Visitor Publishing Division
Our Sunday Visitor, Inc.
200 Noll Plaza
Huntington, IN 46750
1-800-348-2440

ISBN: 978-1-68192-643-8 (Inventory No. T2501)
1. **RELIGION**—Christian Living—Women's Interests.
2. **RELIGION**—Christian Living—Inspirational.
3. **RELIGION**—Christianity—Catholic.

eISBN: 978-1-68192-644-5
LCCN: 2021943295

Cover and interior design: Amanda Falk
Cover art: AdobeStock

PRINTED IN THE UNITED STATES OF AMERICA

For my mom, Helen Dignan, whose constant support, prayer, and love lift me up always. There is no greater example of God's unconditional love here on earth.

Contents

Foreword

Whenever I am leading a women's retreat, and I announce that we will be discussing the Gospel story of Mary and Martha, the women in attendance smile, laugh a little, and exchange some knowing glances. We women love the story of Mary and Martha because it is our story. It's a story that precisely describes a uniquely feminine tension every one of us experiences — the tension between this world and the next, between doing and being.

We women are doers. We all do different things in different ways, but so many of us like ticking off the boxes on our checklists. We like to get things done.

And thanks be to God for good women who do get things done. Thanks be to God for women who change sheets, run meetings, bring casseroles, plan menus, pay bills, make phone calls, fold towels, and drive carpools. We show up. We work hard, even when no one else notices or bothers to say thank you. We women do invaluable work in our homes, families, churches, and communities every day.

In his 1995 *Letter to Women*, Pope St. John Paul II writes: "Necessary emphasis should be placed on the 'genius of women,' not only by considering great and famous women of the past or present, but also those ordinary women who reveal the gift of their womanhood by placing themselves at the service of others in their everyday lives. For in giving themselves to others each day, women fulfill their deepest vocation."

Placing ourselves at the service of others is part of our genius; it's part of our deepest vocation.

With this in mind, we might read the Gospel story of Mary and Martha and, as Claire McGarry initially does, find ourselves quite firmly on Martha's side. Whenever this Gospel passage is read at Mass, my own mother, who raised nine children of her own and now is grandmother to forty-seven and great-grandmother to four and counting, likes to observe: "I know that Mary chose the better part, but I'm pretty sure everyone was glad to have a hot meal at the end of that day."

True enough. And so, how are we to understand Jesus' reprimand of Martha, gentle though it is? Martha herself is so sure that she is correct in her righteous indignation that she scolds Jesus: "Do you not care?" And she brazenly tells him what to do: "Tell her to help me!" We can imagine Martha's surprise at Jesus' response, because it is likely very close to our own. *Umm, what do you mean, Jesus? There is something more important here than the dishes in the sink and the roast in the oven?*

When we are "busy and distracted with many things," the temptation can be to seek our worth in our accomplishments. We might begin to feel as though we can somehow earn our status with God, if only we work hard enough and do enough of the right things.

With his gentle admonishment, what Jesus invites Martha to see, and what he invites each of us to see, is that we are valued just as we are. We can't earn God's love. He loves us and we are worthy simply because we exist. God made each of us and pronounced us good. He loves each of us so much that he just wants to be with us. He longs for us to sit at his feet, and fix our gaze upon him.

Why is it so hard to do that? Why do I sit in the quiet of my living room in the early hours of morning, prayer book in hand, and then struggle as I find my mind flitting from one thought to the next — thoughts about bathrooms that need to be cleaned, emails that need to be written, and deadlines that need to be met? Why is it so hard to sit, be still, and allow God to love us?

I'm not sure any of us can become perfect Marys on this side of heaven, but it is a goal worth striving for, and that is why I am so grateful to Claire McGarry for writing this book. As Jesus does with Martha, Claire calls us by name, gently takes us by the hand, and walks us through a discovery of "the better part."

"Martha, Martha ..." Jesus says, and we can hear the love in his voice as he interrupts her. He wants to interrupt us too. And that's what Claire invites us to see in the pages that lie ahead. By sharing her own struggles and stories, she walks us through the uniquely feminine challenges of learning to trust our intuition, balancing priorities, setting boundaries, navigating change, preventing comparison, asking for help, and taking care of ourselves. In her own, gentle way, Claire invites us to find grace in our tensions, and thus she nudges us toward Jesus. Toward the better part.

I invite you to look for Jesus in the words you are about to read. Let him interrupt you. Listen for his voice, hear him call you by name, and then open your heart to receive the better part, which is nothing less than the gift of God himself, and the love, peace, balance, and lasting joy that can only be found in him.

Danielle Bean

Introduction

Now as they went on their way, he entered a certain village, where a woman named Martha welcomed him into her home. She had a sister named Mary, who sat at the Lord's feet and listened to what he was saying. But Martha was distracted by her many tasks; so she came to him and asked, "Lord, do you not care that my sister has left me to do all the work by myself? Tell her then to help me." But the Lord answered her, "Martha, Martha, you are worried and distracted by many things; there is need of only one thing. Mary has chosen the better part, which will not be taken away from her."
— Luke 10:38–42

In 2014, I began a blog called *Shifting My Perspective*. I wanted to share how my struggles in life are always transformed when

I apply Scripture to them. I thought I chose the name on a whim, but all these years later, it's clear how intentional God was when he laid that name on my heart.

Whenever I look at any problem through the lens of faith and God's Word, my take on it shifts. From that new perspective, I see another side, one that reveals the invaluable lesson I need to learn in that moment. I can't say I always succeed in applying the lessons, but I can say I try. Regardless of my progress (or lack thereof), whenever I bring my issues to God, I always find a wellspring of new hope and joy.

One of the most profound shifts came while I was reading Luke 10:38–42 one morning during my prayer time. It's the story of Jesus' visit to the home of Martha and Mary. As a chronic Martha, I was relating to her completely. I, too, was getting frustrated with her sister, Mary, annoyed that she was just sitting at Jesus' feet, leaving all the work to Martha. I was cheering Martha on as her resentment escalates to such a degree that she confronts Jesus and asks him to tell Mary to help. No matter how many times I read this passage, I want Jesus to turn to Mary and say, "Get up and help her already!" But he never does. Instead, he tells Martha that Mary has chosen the "better part." Jesus doesn't seem to want to take away Martha's tension. He seems to be challenging her in the midst of it.

That's what grace does: It lights a candle in the dark so the gift it holds can come to light.

As I read the passage that morning, I couldn't help but wonder: *Why does Jesus respond like this? If our God is a God of abundant goodness, why doesn't he take Martha's tension — and ours — away? Why doesn't he just smooth over the difficulties so that*

Martha — and we — can lead lives of ease and enjoyment?

That's when it happened. Right when I was questioning why God doesn't take away our struggles, a transformation occurred. In his ever-surprising way, God led me through a process that turned everything upside down. While I was focusing solely on the tension, he was shining a light to illuminate the gift within. That's what grace does: It lights a candle in the dark so the gift it holds can come to light.

Please don't misunderstand me. I'm not saying God gives us problems in order to give us gifts. It's not his style to send us struggles, discord, or disease. We're pretty good at creating many of those sufferings for ourselves, whether individually or collectively, with how we treat ourselves, each other, and our planet. I *am* saying that God wants us to be joyful, and he never, ever gives up on us. No matter how bad any situation is, he always infuses it with good. As Ann Voskamp says in her book *The Greatest Gift: Unwrapping the Full Love Story of Christmas*: "We are not spared of all trials, but we are always spared of the trials that have no gifts."* After that morning in prayer, I now firmly believe that God does place gifts within our struggles. Those gifts are so life-giving, they can turn our tension into grace if we just unwrap them, discover what's inside, and apply them to our lives.

Defining Tension and Its Levels

If we want to find grace in our tension, it's important to understand what tension is. At its root, it's "the state of being stretched," and it's necessary for a whole slew of things. Without it, we couldn't zip up a sweatshirt, fly a kite, or tune a guitar. The type of tension I'm talking about, however, isn't this physical kind; it's the kind that stretches and stirs our emotions, challenging us to respond. If we choose the correct response, the stress dissolves.

---

*Ann Voskamp, *The Greatest Gift: Unwrapping the Full Love Story of Christmas* (Carol Stream, IL: Tyndale House Publishers, 2013), 233.

If we don't, we end up feeding our tension, causing it to grow into a stronger emotion. That's when different levels of tension occur, based on the situation and our response.

Low-level tension is God's gentle nudge, telling us we're reaching our limit. We're about to be stretched too far and veer off course. Had Mary made different choices when Jesus came to visit, perhaps she would have felt this type of pressure. In chapter 1, I'll talk more about this imagined scenario and low-level tension itself. Spoiler alert: When we heed God's gentle nudge and make the proper adjustments in our choices, things smooth out, and we get back on course. In fact, once we realign ourselves, it's almost miraculous how the angst just melts away, leaving us filled with peace and joy. Conversely, if we don't take action when we feel strained, or if we take the wrong action, our bad choices begin to eat us up. That's when we move into mid-level tension.

Mid-level tension occurs when we ignore the warning bells that sound in our hearts when we've chosen wrong. Each time we do, we move further and further away from becoming the person God is calling us to be, and the pressure builds. The more it builds, the more tension consumes us. What begins as an uncomfortable feeling soon becomes a full-blown plethora of negative emotions. This is the zone Martha allows herself to move into. Rather than wondering if she should be doing things differently, she forges on with her choices and allows her emotions to take over. Soon she's feeling downright stressed, resentful, and persecuted. It will take several chapters to explore the different ways so many of us routinely rent space in this domain. As we learn more about mid-level tension, we'll discover how important it is for us to be aware of and receptive to God as he pulls us back into the realm of his grace. It's there that he'll show us the *external* changes we need to make to dissolve the tension.

Finally, high-level tension sets in when we become devastated by circumstances seemingly beyond our control. Whether it's a dreaded diagnosis, financial ruin, or the loss of a loved one, we often feel as if we have no say or choice in this level. As Martha and Mary were devastated by the loss of their brother, Lazarus, in John 11, we can lose hope, peace, and purpose. The final chapters of this book explore the antidote: making the *internal* changes that can transform our hearts and minds. Not only will we see Martha and Mary embrace this concept and transform their own tension into grace; we'll also see in John 12 how they reap the rewards of doing so.

The Transformation Process

I have revisited that morning with God in my prayer more times than I can count. Being a systematic person, I wanted to capture the process of how God had transformed my tension into grace. I knew that if I could do that, I'd be able to dissolve tension every time it came my way. I realize now that, as I sat with God, he first asked me to identify why I get so worked up when I read this Gospel passage about the sisters. He helped me see that I get upset, as Martha does, be-

When we loosen our hold on our emotions, they no longer have a hold on us.

cause I, too, am a doer. In the midst of all my doing, I'm always hoping someone will step up and help. If my sister were just sitting there, watching me run around like a crazy lady, I'd be frustrated too.

God then encouraged me to sit with him with that frustration. Rather than just quickly labeling it and calling it "bad," he challenged me to look it squarely in the eye and feel it. When I did, I felt frustration's power over me diminish. Rather than bottling it up and letting the pressure build, I let it out, and I let it go. I learned, firsthand, that when we loosen our hold on our emotions, they no longer have a hold on us.

It wasn't until my temper cooled that I was able to hear God tell me how he views things. I was getting upset on Martha's behalf because I was being defensive. I was trying to advocate for her being right because that would make me right too. God's approach was so loving, it dismantled my defenses. I could then see what Martha was choosing to postpone. More importantly, I could see what I choose to postpone when living out my Martha tendencies: playing a game with my kids and making memories; going out on a date with my husband and strengthening our bond; spending much-needed time with my friends and reconnecting. In a nutshell, by prioritizing my to-do list, as Martha does, I deprioritize the things that really matter.

Once I understood all this, God inspired me to make the necessary changes in my life. I'll talk more about them as we progress through this book. But even before I implemented a single one of them, I felt empowered. God gave me clear insight into my problem and clear direction on how to fix it. In just twenty minutes of spending time at his feet, he helped me see the gift that was tucked inside all that tension.

The crazy thing is, when I look back over the experience, I realize that the process God led me through spells the word gift.

At his feet, he helped me:

- **G**auge, identify, and name the tension I was feeling
- **I**nvite it in so I could look it in the eye, robbing it of its hold over me
- **F**ilter it through his lens, which sees the whole picture with love
- **T**ransform it by inspiring me to make the necessary

changes in my life and in myself

The impact of that morning's experience in prayer has changed me forever. Now, every time I bump up against stress of any kind, I take it to God. My journal is filled with G-I-F-T entry after G-I-F-T entry. Each and every time, God reveals some amazing gem buried in the struggle I bring to him. As I take each gem and apply it to my life, the tension turns to grace, and the sparkle returns. I feel rejuvenated, empowered, filled with new hope, and excited to move beyond the problem and back into the light. Recognizing the profound impact of this process, I've ended each chapter of this book with a prayer that will bring us to God, and questions for reflection in the G-I-F-T format. Whether you choose to ponder the questions quietly with God, journal your responses to gain further clarity, or discuss them with a trusted friend, I'm certain God will guide you to the grace he has placed within your tension.

Benjamin Franklin said, "Nothing is certain but death and taxes." I'd like to propose that conflict, and its arising stress, should be added to that list of certainties. Tension will always rear its ugly head. Therefore, unless it's going to put us in mortal or spiritual danger, why not move toward it rather than away? Why not shift our perspective and see it as a place for new growth, versus a cross or a curse? Why not use tension as a bridge to reverse our direction when we've chosen the wrong response, crossing back to the place where we can choose again?

I'm not a therapist, but I still long to help you solve your problems. I'm not a theologian, but I still yearn to draw you closer to God. I've finally figured out that if I share this concept of finding grace in tension through the G-I-F-T process, it might motivate you to bring your problems to God. If you do, he'll do the rest. That hope was the entire motivation behind my writing this book. As I wrote, I asked the Holy Spirit to help me find the right words to inspire you to be open to this concept and try this process. If, after you read it, you find yourself at God's feet, unwrapping the gifts in your own tension, my prayer will be answered. Thank you for trusting me to accompany you on this journey.

Blessings and unwrapping the gifts,
Claire

1

Embracing the Gentle Nudge

He entered a certain village, where a woman named
Martha welcomed him into her home. She had a
sister named Mary, who sat at the Lord's feet.
— Luke 10:38–39

A few summers ago, my little family took a boat cruise down the Charles River in Boston. As a special treat, the captain invited my three kids to drive the boat. I guess he deemed them perfectly capable, because he handed them the wheel without any instruction at all. One after the other, they were given complete freedom to steer wherever they wanted. The exception was when we were approaching a bridge.

All the bridges over the Charles River have rather narrow steel arches mounted on concrete pylons. If you don't align a boat correctly, you risk steering it into pure concrete. Obviously, the captain's goal was to prevent my kids from crashing his boat. Only then did he teach them how delicate a rudder is. It needs only the smallest nudge to change the boat's entire trajectory. Based on his years of experience, he knew just how slightly the wheel needs to be turned to realign the boat. He coached my kids accordingly. I wouldn't say they steered that boat straight through the middle of those archways, but by listening to and obeying the captain, my kids did well enough to get us safely through.

Veering Off Course

In the Gospel of Luke, both Martha and Mary want to steer their boats straight and true. They yearn to live their lives well, following Jesus' example as best they can. Doing so, however, is more challenging than it seems. Life routinely requires us to adjust our rudders, and choices come along that tempt us to go off course. Clearly, both sisters are deeply devoted to Jesus and would never intentionally succumb to that temptation. Yet it is possible to make a choice with the right motive, only to go overboard, empowering that choice to steer the ship. Inevitably, that approach takes us adrift.

Despite reading this Gospel passage countless times over the years, it's only recently that I noticed that Martha is alone when she greets Jesus at the door. Of course, it takes only one sentence for Mary to be at his feet. But in that space between the sentences, I wondered what it might have been like for Mary had she not prioritized correctly. What if she, like Martha, chose to show her devotion to Jesus through her time spent in the kitchen? What if she, too, let the busyness of hosting steer her ship? It was the woman's role to serve, after all. It wasn't to be in the company of men, lounging at their feet. What if, right from the start, Mary *had been* doing her part in the preparations? What if she'd been so absorbed in the kitchen that she never made it to Jesus in the living room?

Scripture tells us that isn't the case. But had Mary initially chosen wrong, prioritizing the *doing for* Jesus over the *being with* him, she wouldn't have been steering her boat straight and true for who she is. She'd have handed the wheel over to her to-do list, giving it the power to determine her direction. The thing is, to-do lists don't make very good pilots. They'll always steer us off course when we make them the highest priority in our lives.

Had Mary decided to stay in the kitchen, I believe that choice would have had her looking inward, feeling regret. Where Martha is a reactive person, Mary is a reflective one. I think Mary's personality would have had her fully aware of her emotional state, facing the tension head-on, not running from it. I bet she would have rethought her choice — and quickly.

Our ever-helpful God would have gently nudged Mary to help her see that while she was addressing the many tasks at hand, her compass was broken. He knew

There's no better place to realign ourselves than at the feet of Jesus.

that her heart's true desire was to be with his Son. Had she made the choice to stay in the kitchen, it would have filled her with remorse, pointing her toward a concrete pylon. God wouldn't want her to crash her boat. He'd want her to reclaim the wheel so he could help her get back on track. Of course, there's no better place to realign ourselves than at the feet of Jesus. Were God's gentle prompt necessary, I believe Mary would have embraced it by taking back the wheel and choosing again. Her new choice would have taken her from the kitchen to the living room to be with Jesus.

Whether she is remorseful or not, what we are certain about is that Mary does make it to the feet of Jesus. Yet she must feel some pressure from Martha. Mary knows she has left all the work to her sister. Surely this had to be difficult for her. Mary has such a gentle heart. Despite being in the right place outwardly, could Mary have been conflicted inwardly? What if her heart and mind were in the kitchen, thinking of all that needed to be done? What if she had fallen prey to guilt for leaving all the work to Martha?

Guilt is a powerful emotion. It barricades our hearts and ears, blocking out what we're supposed to hear. Had Mary succumbed to guilt, she would have spent her time at Jesus' feet not listening to a single thing he said, too consumed by her inner tension. Fortunately, that's not the case. In fact, we'll see very clearly that Mary succeeds in aligning her heart and her head with her choice.

Embracing the Gentle Nudge

For those of us who aren't always successful in aligning our hearts with our heads, there's hope. God always shows up in any misalignment and provides a gentle nudge to get us back on course. In Mary's case, had she not been aligned, he would have prompted her to realize she was about to miss out on one of the greatest opportunities of her life: the Son teaching about his Father right in her own living room. His godly perspective would have shown her she had a choice to make: Remain behind the barricade of her guilt, or dismantle it to be showered in the grace of Jesus' teachings.

We all know that when Jesus says, "There is need of only one thing" (Lk 10:42), he's referring to whatever draws us closer to God. What he says next isn't that Mary has chosen the better action. He says she has chosen "the better part." I believe the "better part" isn't just *what* Mary chooses but *how* she chooses. Whether she was in need of God's gentle nudge or not, in the end, Mary chooses to be with Jesus from a place of love, with no shred of guilt in sight. In fact, the *what* and the *how* of her choice are so in harmony that her ears and her heart are open wide. That's why Scripture says she "listened to what he was saying." Listening is an active verb, one we need to be fully present for. In her quiet and unassuming way, Mary illustrates

> *I believe the "better part" isn't just what Mary chooses but how she chooses.*

that in order for any choice to move into the realm of "the better part," we have to carry it out with right intention.

It's said that there are only two root emotions: love and fear. Every other emotion can be traced back to one or the other. If we make a right choice outwardly but do so out of guilt, jealousy, peer pressure, or any other emotion rooted in fear, tension inevitably shows up. When that stress comes to a head, our real motive comes out, obliterating any positive impact our good choice was meant to achieve. It's only when we choose from a place of compassion, humility, generosity, or any other emotion rooted in love that we draw closer to the source of love itself, God. When our hearts and heads are aligned with our right choice stemming from love, not only does tension dissolve but everyone involved is blessed by our choice, ourselves included.

As one who sees into hearts, Jesus knows that when Mary sits at his feet, her entire being is aligned with her choice. She's fully present out of pure love for him, the "better part" of any choice. That's why it can't be "taken away from her" (v. 42). The "better part" always brings a peace so profound, it infuses our soul — a place where that peace is ours to keep forever.

When we embrace the idea that our low-level tension is a gentle nudge from God telling us we've made a wrong choice (or a right choice for the wrong reason), we're more inclined to adjust our choice right away. Doing so prevents us from continuing on a trajectory that takes us further off course the longer we're on it. Embracing this idea with faith also shows us how God can, and will, use everything for our good — tension included. As Romans 8:28 says, "We know that all things work together for good for those who love God, who are called according to his purposes."

In fact, I believe that tension is God's school of second chances. If we choose wrong the first time around, he uses the resulting bad feelings to prompt us back on course. It's all part of the upside-down perspective of faith. Whereas the world sees defeat when Christ hangs on the cross, the eyes of faith see the greatest victory ever won. Whereas the world sees tension as something that can possibly unravel us, the eyes of faith see it as God's opportunity to knit us back together, stronger than before. The eyes of faith see gifts everywhere, even in the midst of the tension.

The heart of faith knows that when tension arises, choosing the better part, sitting at Jesus' feet with our hearts wide open, is the answer. There we'll hear him say: "I can help you through this. Let me show you the gift this struggle holds. Let me teach you how to unwrap it and apply it to your life so you can dissolve your tension. I want to give you a peace and purpose so great, it will bless you beyond measure."

God as Our Captain

Two weeks after my family's boat cruise down the Charles River, my husband and I gave our oldest son, Zack, his first cell phone for the start of high school. I used Zack's experience driving the boat to explain how things were going to work with the phone. I said he was guaranteed to make mistakes; this was new territory for him. Making those mistakes wouldn't make him a bad kid. They'd just be identifying his areas for growth. Additionally, the mistakes he made wouldn't be what formed and defined his character; how he reacted to those mistakes would. My job was to be like the captain, gently nudging him away from any inappropriate choices on the phone to help him correct his behavior. His job was to remain open to my guidance and follow it, just as he did with the captain's.

Things are no different for each one of us. God is our parent and our captain. He has deemed each of us perfectly capable of steering our own boat in life, and he has given us free will to go wherever we see fit. We're guaranteed to make mistakes. However, those mistakes are our growing points. Additionally, the mistakes we make don't form and define us; it's how we react to them that does. Often, we need just slight nudges from God to get us back on track.

Our ever-patient Captain wants to gently guide us through all of our problems and keep us on course. Like my kids driving that boat on the Charles River, we may not draw a straight line with our lives; but when we listen to God and work through our struggles, we'll steer our boats through the tension to enjoy his grace on the other side.

• •

At His Feet
Loving Captain,

Thank you for always using everything for my good, even the tension I feel. Help me to focus on the gifts you are illuminating in my struggle when all I can see is darkness. Give me the strength and courage I need to unwrap those gifts and spend time with them at your feet. Take away my negative emotions so my perspective will shift, allowing me to see the whole picture through your loving eyes. Reveal to me the new choices I need to make in order to diffuse my stress. Encourage and inspire me to carry out those choices so I may experience the peace, purpose, and joy you want to bless me with. Remind me that it's only by remaining open and responsive to your gentle nudges that I'll be able to realign myself with the course you've mapped out for me.

I ask this in Jesus' name. Amen.

———————————

Unwrapping the G-I-F-T

Gauge — Am I feeling any tension that's telling me I'm veering off course? What name would I give that tension?

Invite — What happens when I invite that tension in and sit with it at God's feet?

Filter — What do I see when I look at the situation through the filter of God's loving eyes?

Transform — What change is God inspiring me to make so I can realign and get back on track?

2
Choosing a New Response

… and listened to what he was saying.
— Luke 10:39

When our kids were little and vacations were few and far between, my husband and I took advantage of one of those promotions that require you to sit through a two-hour timeshare presentation in exchange for a very reduced rate on a condo rental. We chose the promotion being offered at a family resort in Vermont. For one whole week, not only were we surrounded by the beauty of the Green Mountain State, but we enjoyed the resort's eight swimming pools, all-day camps for the kids, and babysitting in the evenings. It was phenomenal to go out at night with my husband and be adults! Despite the much-needed freedom it gave us from our children so we could rejuvenate, we did keep them out of camp for a few days so we could bond as a family and participate in some of the activities together.

We McGarrys are a competitive bunch, and we took those family activities very seriously. I'm not kidding when I tell you my husband, John, had the kids stretching out before all the races, whether it was the potato sack race, the three-legged race, or the wheelbarrow run. I'm also not kidding when I tell you I saw him lift whichever child he was tied to, or pushing, so that the child literally levitated. With nothing or no one slowing him down, my husband was able to run us to victory each and every time. The game that stands out most from that vacation is the tug of war.

A tug of war is a contest that requires everyone on a team to work together, or at least that's the premise. As we McGarrys gripped one end of the rope, another unsuspecting family grabbed the other. When the staff member yelled "Go," John took it easy for a while. I watched the red scarf marking the middle of the rope move left, then right, depending on which family was pulling harder at the time. My husband, with his usual patience, watched and waited for the other family to grow weary from flexing their muscles. When he deemed the moment was right, he let his full strength loose, giving a shoulder-wrenching tug that pulled that red scarf well over our winning line.

Resisting the Adjustment

My husband isn't the only one who grabs a rope and gives a shoulder-wrenching tug. Martha uses this tactic too. I believe that in the midst of her initial tension, God gently nudges her to make a change. Rather than listening to what his nudge is saying and adjusting her choices accordingly, she grabs onto the rope of her frustration and pulls it tight. Not possessing the same intuitive skills as her sister, Martha doesn't look inward to see if the problem might lie with her. She looks outward and deems Mary the source of the problem. Martha assumes that if Mary were to adjust her choice and help with the preparations, the tension would naturally dissolve. So Martha digs her heels in deep and gives her own version of a shoulder-wrenching tug by going to Jesus. As if recruiting him for her team, she tries to convince Jesus to tell Mary to change what she's doing. Martha figures that once Jesus is on her side, there's no way they won't succeed in pulling that middle-marking red scarf well over their line. What's really happening, though, is that all that rope pulling and heel digging is causing Martha's tension to increase in pressure, escalating her low-level tension right into the mid-level zone.

When tension rears its ugly head, it's easy to be a Martha and look outward for the source. If we can deem other people or circumstances the root of the problem, we don't have to make any adjustments or changes ourselves. Introspection can be hard and uncomfortable. It's so much easier to avoid it. Yet avoiding it puts us at risk of not listening to God's gentle nudge telling us we're veering off course. We also overlook the fact that making an immediate change in our choices could stop the strain at its lowest level.

Choosing a New Response

When we don't choose a new response in low-level tension, the pressure escalates, driving us right into tension's mid-level zone. Because this happens so often, the following eight chapters will address the most common areas where we're prone to playing the tug of war game. When we tap into the reactive side of ourselves, grabbing the rope of tension and pulling it tight, we wreak havoc in innumerable ways. Rather than choosing a new response, we dig our heels into the choices we're making, and give a shoulder-wrenching tug to get our way. The more we pull, the tighter the rope gets. The tighter the rope gets, the more tension is created. As we watch that red scarf move back and forth with the push and pull of our reluctance to change, we get more focused on winning the game than on the toll it's taking on our lives.

This happens most when our Martha-like tendencies have us fixating on *doing* rather than on *being,* succumbing to the way the world defines success and progress rather than how God does. The end result is we fall head first into the productivity trap.

> *Trying to do enough in order to be enough, we keep grabbing that rope and pulling it with all our might.*

Trying to do enough in order to be enough, we keep grabbing that rope and pulling it with all our might. As we continue down the wrong path, or the right path with the wrong intention, our resentment mounts, putting us at risk of stretching ourselves beyond our capabilities. Yet, unlike most games in which both sides get competitive, we don't realize it's a one-sided match, and we are doing all the pulling.

As patient as my husband can be in his gaming strategy, he's no match for God. God has no need to flex his muscles nor a desire to pull us to him against our will. He will wait an eternity for us, despite our resistance. All the while, he gently holds on to his side of the rope, yearning to remain connected to us. As he watches us grow weary from flexing our muscles, instead of giving a shoulder-wrenching tug, he whispers that he wants to help. His whisper is meant to inspire us to lean into him and listen to what he has to say. That's how we hear him suggest a new response, one that's right for us, one that will dissolve all our stress and angst. He also patiently waits for us to choose him.

When we don't, and our wrong choices continue to pull us away from peace and joy, and away from him, he patiently remains within the tension, sending love down the line, hoping we'll eventually get the message that something's not right, that we need to make a change.

Playing the Blame Game

Another memory I have from our vacation in Vermont is the afternoon John and I rented Segways. To an observer, it looks as if riding the self-balancing, scooter-like machine involves standing on the platform over the two wheels and using the handlebars to steer. Not so. The handlebars are just accessories to hold on to, to make you feel more secure. All the commands to the personal transporter are given through the distribution of your weight. If you want to move forward, you lean forward. If you want to go backward, you lean back. If you want to turn right, you lean right. If you want to turn left, you lean left. In order to stop, you stand straight. The more concise explanation is: How you lean determines where you end up. Said that way, it sounds so much easier than it is.

While John did well, I spun in circles, drove off the smooth trail into the rocky hillside, and went backward when I wanted to stop. I'm accustomed to learning new things quickly, and I don't handle failure well. Consequently, my frustration continued to mount as I fumbled like a toddler learning to walk. The good news is, we had a guide all to ourselves who really knew his stuff. By focusing solely on us, he was able to determine what I was doing wrong and how I needed to adjust to fix it. In retrospect, had I been more open to his instruction, I would have learned more quickly. But my ego was bruised. I didn't want to admit I was at fault, nor did I want to have to work at something that looked so easy. I was on vacation, after all. So I switched tactics. I decided to place the blame on my Segway. I claimed it wasn't balanced correctly and was reading my signals wrong. Even though our guide wasn't buying it, I kept pulling on my rope of frustration, like Martha, and digging my heels in (which is probably why I kept going backward when I wanted to stop!). Without a doubt, my approach made things worse.

How you lean determines where you end up.

As we journey through the following section on mid-level tension, we'll learn, through Martha, how a refusal to change makes matters worse. We end up feeding our tension when we should be starving it. We'll also learn that it's usually our *external* actions that cause tension to escalate into the mid-level zone. Likewise, it's usually an *external* change that God is prompting us to make to transform that tension into grace, getting us back to the better part.

••

At His Feet
Devoted Guide,

Help me to feel your gentle nudge telling me something's not right. When I do recognize it, keep me from looking outward to place the blame. Remind me that you never ask me to judge anyone else; I'm solely responsible for my own behavior. Fill me with the understanding that when I am at fault, your purpose is never to shame me into feeling worse. You see the peace-filled life I could lead if only I'd listen to you, and you long to have me experience that. Inspire me to embrace the idea that when you do highlight a problem, it's to motivate me to make the change that will dissolve my tension. Give me the humility I need to lay down my ego so I can listen to all you're whispering into my heart.

Once I hear you, give me the fortitude, grace, and wisdom to carry out the changes you're inspiring me to make. Keep me mindful that you are always there beside me, every step of the way. Increase my trust, knowing that when you're on my team and I follow your lead, you always bring me to victory.

I ask this in Jesus' name. Amen.

———————————

Unwrapping the G-I-F-T

Gauge — When things aren't going smoothly, do I typically listen for God's gentle nudge that tells me the change I need to make? Or am I inclined to place the blame elsewhere, pulling the rope of my tension tighter? What feelings usually result from that approach?

Invite — What happens when I invite those feelings in and sit with them at God's feet?

Filter — What do I see when I look at the situation through the filter of God's loving eyes?

Transform — What changes do I need to make so I don't grab tension's rope, making things worse by pulling it tight?

3
Drawing Healthy Boundaries

But Martha was distracted ...
— Luke 10:40

When I served as a missionary for three years in Guatemala, one of the first things I noticed when I got to my village was that all the fences were made out of barbed wire. I'm from New England, the land of Norman Rockwell and the white picket fence. I was used to ornate structures that were more about aesthetics than they were about creating an enclosure. But that's First World living. Third World living is all about the cheapest thing that meets the need.

Sure enough, barbed-wire fences are the cheapest way to

define property lines. They also keep animals in and any "un-wanteds" out. Unfortunately, they do so in a harsh and unfriend-ly manner. If you brush up against them or try to lean on one, you're left with slashes, cuts, and wounds.

When I think of boundaries now, those fences still come to mind. Although a fence does make a great visual when explain-ing the concept of personal boundaries, you may want to imagine one of the white picket kind. We should never construct anything in our lives out of something that cuts or harms others.

Like the fences in our yards, boundaries should run along the property lines of our lives.

Instead, personal boundaries should be used to politely define our priorities and our limits. They also mark and separate where one thing ends and another be-gins. Like the fences in our yards, boundaries should run along the property lines of our lives. When we use wise discernment in draw-ing them, they define and sepa-rate what matters to us from what doesn't; what we're responsible for from what we're not; what's enough to give from what's too much; what behavior we're willing to accept from what we should not; whom we let into our lives from whom we should not. There's almost no limit to the number of limits we should draw in our lives.

Lacking Limits

Martha's boundaries seem clear and defined when we first meet her in Luke 10. By placing herself at the door to *welcome* Jesus "into her home" (v. 38), not only does Martha position herself to draw closer to Jesus, but she does so with right intention. Otherwise, Luke would have said she "opened the door" or "let him in." In Martha's welcome, we picture her fully present. She greets and honors this man who is more than just her brother Lazarus's friend. He's *her* friend too.

The next mention of Martha, however, has her "distracted by her many tasks" (v. 40). Again, Luke chooses his words carefully. *Distracted* conveys that Martha is no longer present to Jesus. That would be fine if she found meaning in her tasks, making them a gift for him as she works in the kitchen. Someone has to prepare the meal, after all. But Luke's choice of *distracted* clearly conveys that's not the case.

With so little said about Martha, we'll never know whether she usually drew healthy boundary lines for herself. If, when preparing for guests, she did define the line between "good enough" and "too much," it appears that she has lost sight of it during this visit. That's the thing with boundaries: Once they're drawn, they need to be routinely patrolled to guard against a breach — by us or by others. Even if Martha had drawn healthy boundaries, they clearly don't hold up on this occasion. Her many tasks find the hole in the fence and charge right in. The end result is that her heart is no longer in the right place, and her idea of what's necessary no longer fits the situation.

All the while, Mary just sits at Jesus' feet, listening to all he has to say. Martha may not be taking the time to sit at Jesus' feet, but she's well aware of the time Mary is spending there. And because the blurred boundary lines have Martha expecting too much of herself, she turns those same expectations on her sister, causing the pressure to mount. For each minute Mary is not helping her, the tension time bomb inside Martha ticks closer to exploding. Never once does Martha stop and ask herself whether her expectations for herself or her sister are healthy or necessary. Nor does she notice that Jesus isn't making a single demand of her or of her preparations. That's what happens when our boundaries are misdrawn or missing: We overlook what's really required and wrongly determine what is.

We Marthas struggle when it comes to defining boundaries. As doers and dreamers, we think the sky's our limit. So, more often than not, we skip the boundary-making process altogether. If that's not our reason, there are plenty more: It feels too harsh to define limits with people; we've never been taught how; we're not aware it's our responsibility; someone early on in our lives convinced us that our limits weren't worthy of respect; and so on.

Drawing Healthy Boundaries

Whatever our reason for not defining our personal boundaries, the Bible affirms just how important the process is. In Genesis 1, we read, step by step, how God himself drew boundary lines when he created the world. It's his way of teaching us to do the same. In the beginning, the earth was a "formless void." Knowing how beautiful it could be if only clear lines were established, God separated the light from the darkness, the water from the sky, and the oceans from dry land (see Gn 1:1–10).

In his infinite wisdom, he knew to put "Define boundaries" as item #1 on his to-do list. Tackling them first created order for everything that followed. Just imagine, for a moment, how different things would be if God created animals and man *before* distinguishing light from darkness, water from sky, and oceans from dry land. It would be utter chaos, with the animals and man floundering for a place to stand.

The same holds true on a smaller scale in our lives when we skip the critical step of defining our personal boundaries. We're left fumbling, unsure of our own footing. We get completely confused as to why up feels like down, or why we're swimming against a current, when all we want to do is go for a stroll on dry land.

To follow God's step-by-step approach, we should build our

boundaries as we would any fence, be it picket or stockade. First, we dig the holes for the posts. As we all know, the strength of any fence lies in its posts. If the holes aren't dug deep enough or they're dug in ground that constantly shifts, the posts won't hold up. The same holds true for our personal boundary lines. We need to discern for ourselves what our top priorities are and then dig those posts deep into our daily lives. The more fixed and focused we make them, the more our actions and choices will flow from them.

As our actions and choices flow from them, we learn whether our priorities are healthy. A healthy priority always leads to peace and purpose. For example, if one of our posts is "prioritizing family and friends," we'll put them first, making room for them in our days and our hearts. The resulting joy tells us we've chosen well. If we claim to value kindness and generosity, we'll weave them both into the pattern of our lives. When we feel deep satisfaction in how we treat others, it's confirmation that we've succeeded. Conversely, an unhealthy priority always leads to tension and angst. For example, if we determine that one of our posts is "doing it all," we'll continuously strive, always feeling like less when others accomplish more. If we deem money is all-important, it will color every decision we make, enslaving us to an insatiable greed to always earn more. Whenever a priority or boundary fills us with tension, it's a prompt that tells us it's time to let that priority go.

Whenever a priority or boundary fills us with tension, it's a prompt that tells us it's time to let that priority go.

Once we've established and kept only the priorities that are healthy, we need to connect them. As fencing rails connect the posts to enclose and protect a certain space, our limits are what we use to connect and protect our priorities. Limits are the lines that we draw between what is enough and what is too much. Even a healthy priority can be taken too far.

Martha illustrates how a good priority can be taken to an extreme. The post each sister digs is clear by the action that flows from it. Mary prioritizes *being with* Jesus by sitting at his feet. Martha prioritizes *doing for* him by being in the kitchen. Both are honorable priorities if done with right intentions. But tension comes in when Martha loses sight of the line between enough tasks and too many. What was a healthy boundary for her tips over into the unhealthy zone.

Another way we risk having unhealthy boundaries is if we don't do the work of discerning our priorities ourselves. That's when we make ourselves vulnerable to other people or circumstances drawing them for us. Others don't always have our best interests at heart. When they don't, and we allow them to define things for us, we're left living within the labels and expectations they hem us in with.

God would never hem us in. He doesn't restrict us, nor does he label us. Instead, he's like the best house guest we could ever ask for: He comes only when invited and stays for only as long as he's welcome. And oh, how he yearns for the invitation. Like any loving parent, his desire to be included in our lives is deep and constant. He knows our needs and desperately wants to provide for them. So he waits on the sidelines, hoping we'll turn to him so he can envelop us with all we need and more.

When we do invite him in, we recognize and feel the grace that flows into our lives. If we prioritize him above all else, making him the corner post of our lives, he becomes the point from which all our actions and choices emanate, and the support on which everything hinges. We become anchored in his strength, and no storm or catastrophe can break us. Like a perfect land survey, he reveals the exact topography, grade, and measure of who we are and the limits that work best for us. That's how we learn to detect when anyone encroaches on our boundaries or pushes us too far. With such knowledge, we also become mindful of the blessings in our lives and we're able to nurture them, causing our grass to grow greener. Suddenly, we're so grateful for what we have there's no need to covet what's in anyone else's yard. Instead, we're inspired to help others flourish where they're planted, knowing that's how we build God's kingdom here on earth.

Monitoring Our Boundary Lines

That being said, those of us who are homeowners know that everything requires maintenance. It's important to routinely inspect our boundary lines to make sure they hold. There will always be situations and people challenging our limits. Being aware of those challenges is half the battle of maintaining the lines. In her article "10 Ways to Build and Preserve Better Boundaries," Margarita Tartakovsky, M.S., references Dana Gionta, Ph.D.'s idea that feelings of "discomfort and resentment" are "red flags" that our boundaries are being pushed. Gionta suggests that we rate our feelings of discomfort and resentment on a scale from one to ten. If we place them in the five to ten range, we need to take action to correct the situation.*

I believe that the feeling of loss of control should be added to the list of red flag feelings. For those of us who are like Martha, the need for control is one of our major character traits. Losing control usually leads to our discomfort and resentment. When others won't play by our rules, we get defensive and bitter. Or, when the finish line in the "striving race" gets moved (by us or

---

*Margarita Tartakovsky, M.S., "10 Ways to Build and Preserve Better Boundaries," Psych Central, https://psychcentral.com/lib/10-way-to-build-and-preserve-better-boundaries.

someone else), our patience wears thin, and our tempers grow sharp. Desperate to regain control, we lash out at those around us.

Yet even red-flag feelings of tension can be gifts if we look at them the right way. They're an indication that we need to go to God and work through the G-I-F-T process with him. The Master Architect knows how to build. He also knows how to dismantle. Post by post, he'll remove the emotional barriers confusing the situation so we'll be able to see exactly what's going on and what we need to do about it.

In her loss of control, the red flag of resentment tells Martha she needs to stop, assess her limits, and discover if and what changes need to be made. Obviously, she has taken on too much, pushed herself too far. She can't see that yet, but she can see that Jesus is the one to go to for help. In the upcoming chapters, we'll see how he responds to give her what she truly needs.

Subtle but Clear

I grew up in a neighborhood with a bunch of kids. On any given summer night, there might be ten to twenty of us out playing Buffalo Tag. Buffalo Tag is a game in which, once you're tagged, you join the ranks of those who are "it" and charge after those who have yet to be tagged. Even though the last person standing is declared the winner, he or she is still hunted down by the entire group. That's when you realized the game is aptly named. If you're the last to be tagged, the thunder of feet chasing you sounds like a stampede of buffalo. When you hear it, you run for your life!

This was in an age well before landscaping companies and manicured lawns were the norm. The average yard in our neighborhood was just a sea of weeds and dirt, a direct result of all those kids at play. But not the Itzos'. Our next-door neighbors had a corner lot and a lawn like a green carpet. Mr. and Mrs. Itzo spent hours with fertilizers and sprinklers, caring for their yard with love and two green thumbs. They were so proud of that emerald expanse, they wouldn't put a fence around it. That would block the view. So they erected their boundaries with their will and asked us all not to run on their lawn.

Wow, was it hard to be chased by a horde of kids and have to circle around the Itzos' yard, when cutting straight through it would have been the perfect escape. But we respected the Itzos and what they valued. So circle their yard we did, at least most of the time. There was always that occasion when someone got swept up in the moment and charged across as quickly as possible. That's when Mr. Itzo would come out and reestablish the rule in his kind, yet firm manner. It was clear he'd been watching, monitoring his perimeter, knowing that Buffalo Tag is a boundary pusher for sure.

As challenging as it was to abide by the Itzos' boundaries, I think we kids appreciated how clear they were. We never had to wonder where the line was drawn. With the other neighbors, it was always a guessing game. Sometimes we'd get yelled at for barreling through their yards, and other times not. The confusion was stressful. Not so with the Itzos. There was something very freeing about knowing their clear expectations. It was far easier for us to abide by them, even while running wild.

. . . .

At His Feet

Master Architect,

You were the first to create boundary lines, and what you drew you called "good." Show me how to define and draw boundaries in my life to support who I am in your eyes and who you're calling me to be.

As I dig the posts of my priorities into the soil of my life, remind me to include you as my corner post, rooting myself in your deep wisdom and boundless love. Give me your insight so that, with every priority I have, I'll be able to define the line between enough and too much. As I connect my posts with my limits, help me to do so clearly yet graciously, so that others will accept and respect them. As I live within those parameters, make me mindful of all you've blessed me with so I may nurture it, causing it to grow green and lush. Rather than peering over and coveting what others have, inspire me to encourage and assist others where I can. It's by tending to my own life, and helping others, that I make my corner of the world a better place for all.

I ask this in Jesus' name. Amen.

———————————

Unwrapping the G-I-F-T

Gauge — Have I defined my priorities and dug them deep into my life? Have I established limits for my priorities so I'm moderate in how I protect them? Have I included God as a corner post? Are any of my borders being challenged or pushed? If so, what red-flag feelings of tension are telling me so?

Invite — What happens when I invite those feelings in and sit with them at God's feet?

Filter — What do I see when I look at the situation through the filter of God's loving eyes?

Transform — What boundary lines is God inspiring me to draw for myself? How do I go about making the changes they require? Is God inspiring me to redraw some boundary lines with others? If so, how should I do so?

4
Trimming Back the Extras

By her many tasks.
— Luke 10:40

When my daughter Jocelyn was ten, she had her first gymnastics competition. In preparation, she laid a straight line of duct tape across our family-room rug to simulate a balance beam. Over and over again, she practiced her routine, trying to focus on that line, not veering off, not looking into the kitchen nor out the window in distraction. I watched her try to keep her body and movements straight, her core centered and balanced. It brought me back to my own days of gymnastics when I was her age.

I had the dream of becoming an Olympic gymnast. My favorite and strongest event was the floor. On that forty-square-foot span of cushioned mat, I did my best to run, tumble, dazzle, and wow with my tricks and flips. I also loved the uneven bars and was OK at the vault. I knew I could get better at both if I just worked harder. But put me up four feet high, on a four-inch-wide balance beam, and it was a completely different story. No matter how much I practiced on a slab of wood lying on the ground in my backyard, once I got up on a real balance beam, fear took over. It was a challenge to put one foot in front of the other. I kept looking down from that height and imagining all the ways I could hurt myself if I fell. Rather than working through my fear, finding my center, and keeping myself balanced, I wanted the balance beam to be eliminated as a gymnastic event. It made perfect sense, in my childish mind, to eliminate what was limiting me.

If you've watched the Olympics recently, you'll know I wasn't successful in my master plan. The balance beam is most assuredly one of the four required events for all gymnasts. Truth be told, my plan never went beyond a suppressed desire. I knew, deep down inside, that my expectation was unrealistic: Gymnastics is what it is. No matter how hard I tried, I knew I wasn't going to get my way.

Wanting It All

In Luke 10, Martha not only wants her way but she wants her way by having it all. Luke speaks of Martha's "many tasks," which tells us Martha isn't going for just the bare essentials when Jesus and his disciples come for dinner. She doesn't want any restrictions put on the tricks she has up her sleeve for entertaining. She wants to wow and dazzle by using every square inch to run about, tumble, and flip, from kitchen to living room and back again. She knows her strength lies in serving with a flair, and she knows she can be even better if she just works harder. In fact, I envision her looking around and finding more things she can do, not fewer. Way down deep in her heart and mind, she does plan on spending quality time with Jesus so she can listen to all he has to say. But that ribbon isn't awarded until the routine is finished and the anthem has been played.

So, with her muscles straining and her sanity pushed to the limit, she piles on more. She isn't seeing clearly; logic is escaping her. There's only so much room on any given plate. Yet Martha keeps filling hers, never removing anything to make the necessary space. Even though she's not on a four-inch-wide beam of wood, the additional tasks she keeps taking on are taking her more and more off balance, positioning her for a fall.

> *There's only so much room on any given plate. Yet Martha keeps filling hers, never removing anything to make the necessary space.*

We Marthas are all gymnasts. As members of the More-Is-Better Club, we're always in training to score a perfect ten. In fact, what we're really striving for is membership in the Even-More-Must-Be-Even-Better Club. We're visionaries, and what visions of grandeur we have! If the Marys of this world could have just a glimpse of how we know things can be done, they'd surely subscribe to our club.

Perhaps we think we're savvier than Martha is in this scenario. *We* know when our plates are getting too full. *We* recognize the triggers of stress and tension that tell us we're reaching our limit. *We've* learned that the red flags of impatience and tight muscles in our necks tell us we have changes to make. Far too often, though, we remove the wrong things in order to make space. We eliminate self-care to have more time to get things done. We sleep less, seeing rest as the balance beam restricting our ability to show off our gifts. We postpone spending quality time with those we love, considering them the gold medal we'll win when the event is done. Clearly, we're using the wrong tools to identify which extras, if any, need to be trimmed back. In the process, our stress levels surge far higher than our tricks will ever take us.

Jesus is trying to inspire her to remove some of her many tasks so there will be room for her to add her heart when serving him.

Jesus had it in his power to perform his own tricks. As someone who walked on water, he could have done gravity-defying stunts on a narrow plank of wood up in the air. Yet he didn't because he knew they would be extras that weren't necessary for his purpose. They might have borne fruit in attracting some people to God. But those people would be the type who constantly demand signs to believe. He wants to draw people to God with a true faith — one that believes without seeing. So he focuses on his one, true purpose, using a different beam of wood to atone for our sins and centering us all in his Father in the process. He wants to center Martha in God too.

That's the motivation behind his response to her. It's not her tasks he takes issue with. He's a realist. He knows there are certain things that need to get done. The problem is the quantity of Martha's tasks. It's the excess that's throwing her into an unbalanced state. Jesus is trying to inspire her to remove some of her *many* tasks so there will be room for her to add her heart when serving him.

The *many* tasks in our own lives are pulling us off balance too, preventing us from giving our hearts with right intention. As my spiritual director, Sr. Margretta Flanagan, says, "Excess in one area of our life takes away the ability to grow in another."

Trimming Back the Extras

If you've ever cared for a plant, you know that a wilting flower or branch still draws on the plant, reducing its ability to thrive. When that branch is trimmed, the plant's growth is stimulated. This concept applies to our lives as well. In fact, we daydream all the time about how life would be so much easier if we didn't have so much to do. We know we were made to thrive. We just can't seem to get there on our own.

Jesus wants to help. He wants us to flourish and bloom. We just need to spend time at his feet to hear him tell us which extras we should trim back. He'll also show us the right tools for doing so and how to use them.

One of the best tools is mentioned in Alexandra Kuykendall's book *The Artist's Daughter: A Memoir*. In it, Kuykendall tells her boss, with tears and trepidation, that she's pregnant and needs to pull back from work. Her boss wisely responds, "Do what only you can do."* Reading this quickly, we presume it says, "Do only what you can do." Yet it doesn't. The word order makes a profound difference. "Do *only* what you can do" implies we can try to do it all, but eventually we'll hit a limit. "Do what *only you* can do" coaches us to undertake just what's intended for us. We aren't meant to do it all. It's egotistical of us to think we are. As Kuykendall goes on to say, "God wasn't calling me to do everything. He was calling me to do certain things."

God has gifted each of us with different skills and talents.

---

*Alexandra Kuykendall, *The Artist's Daughter: A Memoir* (Grand Rapids, MI: Revell, 2013), 207.

Our God-ordained tasks tend to be rooted in them. When we understand that God never asks us to be a square peg in a round hole, we begin to see there's a difference between a task meant for us and a task meant for someone else. Asking ourselves the simple question: *Am I the only one who can _____?* clearly defines which tasks are meant for us and which ones are not.

For the tasks that are meant for us, it's important to draw boundaries around them, defining the line between what's necessary and what's excessive in how we carry them out. To do so, we can ask ourselves: *Is _____ really necessary for me to complete this task?* If the answer is yes, we need to ask: *What can I cut out to make room for this?* Like athletes who replay tapes of their performances in order to improve, sometimes it's easier to critique ourselves after the fact in order to see how we can cut back in the future.

For the tasks that aren't meant for us, we need to decline with the Sacred No. If we don't, those tasks will pull us off balance. Time is as precious as money, and our choices come at a price. If taking on another task is going to leave us overdrawn, we have to decline graciously. More importantly, as Kuykendall goes on to infer, we could be robbing someone else of his or her opportunity to shine by taking on his or her God-ordained task. Although the Martha side of us feels tremendous guilt in saying no, when we do so with grace and honesty, we empower others to pursue what could be their better part.

That's exactly what Jesus wants for Martha. He knows that if he can help her see what extras need to be trimmed back, she won't be worried and distracted anymore. That's how she'll thrive and bloom. That's how she'll live out her own better part.

Going for the Gold

When my daughter began gymnastics, her coach spotted her on the balance beam. With each step Jocelyn took, her coach moved right along beside her, with a hand at the ready should Jocelyn lose her balance. That's how my daughter found her confidence and discovered her center of balance. She didn't achieve either on her own.

When it comes to balance in our lives, Jesus is our coach. He doesn't want us to go it alone. He also doesn't want us to settle for silver or bronze. He knows the gold is mastering the balance beam of centering ourselves in God, with all our efforts moving in a straight line to him. Jesus doesn't want us running about on our forty-square-feet of craziness, like the Israelites wandering the desert for forty years, never entering the promised land, never feeling fulfilled. Jesus knows that the way for us to achieve more is by taking on less.

God has created a balance beam specific to each one of us, sanding it smooth and varnishing it until it gleams. He wants to take us to a higher height, and he can, if we take his hand and climb up. As we move forward, tentative step by tentative step, he'll reveal the to-dos only we can do and how to execute them with steady movements to keep us centered. He'll also make it known what unnecessary tasks are draining our resources and need to be cut away. Working with Jesus as our coach, we'll achieve the balance we need for the journey. The more we progress, the more we'll welcome God's trimming back the areas of our lives that could be more fruitful if we just did them differently. When we follow his guidance, not only will we wow and dazzle with the way we thrive, but we'll achieve the gold: room on our plate to sit down to dinner with him and all those we love.

• •

At His Feet
Divine Coach,

Despite my best intentions, I routinely take on too much,

putting myself at risk for a fall. I long to flourish and thrive for you and for all whom I love. When I am unbalanced in my many tasks, and my stress level surges with all my tricks and running about, help me to embrace the idea that I can achieve more by taking on less. Show me what I can cut out and what can be trimmed back. Give me the discernment I need to know which tasks are the ones *only I* can do, and give me the strength and the words to graciously say no to the ones that aren't. Inspire me to take your hand as you lead me to higher heights, to live a life where there's room enough on my plate to include my heart when serving you and when serving others.

I ask this in Jesus' name. Amen.

Unwrapping the G-I-F-T

Gauge — Are there any areas in my life where I'm guilty of having too many tasks? How does that unbalanced state make me feel? What names would I give those emotions?

Invite — What happens when I invite those feelings in and sit with them at God's feet?

Filter — What do I see when I look at the situation through the filter of God's loving eyes?

Transform — What are the tasks that *only I* can do? What extras can I cut out when doing them? What things am I doing that could possibly be God-ordained for someone else? Where can I practice saying the Sacred No, graciously declining when asked to take on more?

5

Deferring to a Different Season

So she came to him and asked.
— Luke 10:40

One of the jobs I had before getting married was working as a job trainer at a grant-funded, welfare-to-work program. As you can imagine, it didn't pay well. I wanted to live on my own, but I knew I couldn't afford an apartment on that meager salary. I settled for renting a room in an old Victorian house with five other people. There were three bathrooms to share, but only one kitchen and living room. I imagined it was going to be like my college days, when the common areas were always a mess, and this Martha would be left to clean them up. Surprisingly, my roommates were never around. They were either out of the house or in their bedrooms, leaving the kitchen and living room virtually unused.

Although that sounds great — getting almost an entire house to myself for very low rent — the pendulum swung too far. There was no sign of anyone's touch to warm up the common spaces. They felt sterile and cold. Needing to always bloom where I'm planted, I started going to the discount flower shop every week to buy the cheapest flowers they had. I'd then place them in empty iced-tea bottles and scatter them around the house. It's amazing how much warmth and beauty fresh-cut flowers can bring to any space, even if they're in recycled bottles. With every new batch I placed around the house, the common areas came to life a little more, inspiring the six of us roommates to spend time together there. As I felt the seeds of friendship taking root, I became more determined than ever to keep up my fresh-cut-flower campaign.

Each week, the prices for various flowers fluctuated. I'm no botanist, but even I figured out it was all about the timing. If a flower was in season, it was available in bulk at a cheaper price. If it was out of season, there were fewer of them, and their price was higher. Some of the more exotic flowers could be special-ordered, costing well beyond what I could afford. I had no choice but to choose the cheapest flowers of the moment.

Doing It Right Now

Martha is no cheap-flower-of-the-moment girl. She has assembled an exotic bouquet of tasks she wants to complete for her dinner party for Jesus, and she wants to do them all right now. Never once does she calculate the cost of what she's trying to achieve. She loves and honors Jesus so much that all she takes stock of is her desire to create warmth and beauty in her home for him. How could anyone fault her for that?

We're not told what season of life Martha is in, but Jesus' visit to her home is such a special moment, it is its own particular season. Perhaps there were things that could have waited or been deferred to a later time. Doing so would have created the time and space she needed to do what was truly necessary and be available to Jesus. Although she's out of sync with her timing, she instinctively knows that any time is a perfect time to go to Jesus for help. He's always available, at no cost at all. Furthermore, Jesus makes himself wholly approachable, even when he's busy talking with the disciples in her living room. When Mary doesn't help Martha, and Martha begins to wilt under the pressure of all she's trying to achieve, she goes to Jesus. Her intention is to place a special order with him to get exactly what she wants. In so many words, she demands that he tell her sister to get up right away and help with everything on her agenda. Martha has no idea the high price she'll pay if Jesus fulfills her request.

We Marthas try to create a greenhouse of our lives where we can control the climate and force what we want to grow, when we want it. We don't consult the *Farmer's Almanac* to determine whether it's the right time for all the to-dos on our lists. We just focus and work harder to create the environment we need for our plans to come to fruition. Our hearts are typically in the right place — most of what's on our list would benefit others if we could pull it all off. Thinking our good intentions should be sufficient fertilizer for the soil of our efforts, we get impatient when things don't grow fast enough. Worse yet, we move from annoyed to angry when things don't grow at all. As our tension rises, we tend to our lives with resentment, ripping out what's not thriving, never noticing how much we bruise those whose roots are entwined with ours.

Like Martha, we go to God and place our special order. Instead of honoring the seasons he's created in our lives, we try to find the right words to convince him to make an exception for us. We want what we want, and we want it now! We never stop to consider the timing of what we're asking for. If we did, we'd realize that some of our requests are like asking for tulips to grow and bloom in January in snowy New England. Their beauty would never see the light of day. All their efforts to put forth their shoots would be met with a hard, icy surface that wouldn't relent, no matter how hard they pushed.

But we're used to pushing, striving, and investing more effort to overcome the obstacles. We grow to think doing so is the natural order of things. So why shouldn't tulips bloom in snow? It's not until we stop and listen to the Creator that we begin to understand the reason for the seasons.

Deferring to a Different Season

All of creation has a woven-in need to rest and rejuvenate. The seasons are God's way of forcing nature to pause for a time each year and simply receive his blessings, like a natural Sabbath. When we try to force nature to skip over this critical part of the cycle, the soil is stripped of its nutrients. What's planted doesn't thrive.

When we don't abide by the seasons in our lives, our resources get depleted, and our joy erodes.

The same thing happens to us. When we don't abide by the seasons in our lives, our resources get depleted, and our joy erodes. We need to model our lives after the farmers who rotate their fields. Exodus 23:10–11 says, "For six years you shall sow your land and gather in its yield; but the seventh year you shall let it rest and lie fallow." When we allow certain areas of our lives to remain fallow and uncultivated for a time, the soil is replenished, making it fertile again. When that rejuvenated field is finally planted, the end result is a quality harvest.

Jesus came down from heaven to reap a quality harvest for God. In doing so, he had to abide by the seasons his Father set forth for him. For thirty years, Jesus patiently waited for his public ministry to begin. That had to be difficult. He knew he had the power to heal, and his heart must have been bursting with the words he wanted to share about his Father's love. Still, Jesus waited. Like a seed that has to germinate, growing roots before it breaks through the soil, he humbly honored his Father's timing, ensuring that he was firmly rooted in, and strengthened by, the Source.

When Jesus' season for preaching and teaching finally arrived, he branched out and performed miracles. He always told the recipients to go in peace and not tell anyone about the miracles. Despite Jesus spreading the Word, he didn't want anyone spreading the word about the miracles he performed. It wasn't his season for glory yet. That season would come much later, after he gave up his life for us and then rose from the dead.

Jesus knows his season of teaching about his Father won't last forever. While he's visiting at Martha's house, he longs for her to sit at his feet and listen to all he has to say before it's too late. He knows her special order to make her sister get up and help is an out-of-season request, one that won't lead to Martha's fruitfulness. Jesus knows that by giving Martha what she wants, he won't be giving her what she needs. She wants help preparing what she plans to feed him. What she needs is to be fed at his feet in preparation for God's plan for her. There, the soil of her heart will be replenished, making her in-season tasks flourish when the time is right.

Nature has yet another way to help in-season things flourish. It uses what's been shed during the off season to further replenish the soil for what's to come. I witnessed this firsthand with the prayer path our parish built on the grounds of our church. A wonderful woman, Mary Ellen, stepped forward to plant and maintain the flower beds around it. She taught me that it's important to keep the fall leaves on the flower beds to insulate them during the cold winter. Although the leaves have been discarded by the trees, they still serve the purpose of protecting and nourishing what's underneath.

Likewise, God will use whatever tasks we lay down now to nourish and protect what he wants to grow in us later. He's planted joy and a specific purpose within each of us. If we don't feel them thriving, we might have too many things vying for our resources. Deferring what isn't in season doesn't mean we can't pick it back up in the future. By laying down certain tasks for a time, we provide space and resources for what's meant to grow in this season and protect what's meant to grow in the next. When we adhere to the process, we work in harmony with God's timing, starving tension and the weeds that feed on it.

There are seasons for our expectations too. When we don't align what we expect of ourselves and others with our current circumstances, it's like watering our stress with Miracle Grow. Our stress grows faster and stronger than ever before. Expecting a toddler always to behave, for example, or thinking we'll serve a well-balanced meal every night while working full-time sets us up for failure. It's only by matching our expectations to our present reality that we have any hope of keeping our joy intact.

Recognizing the timing in our present reality can be challenging. Unlike packaged food with a sell-by date, or a seed packet with the planting season printed on it, the timing in our lives is not so clear-cut. We need to take time in prayer to discern what can wait and what cannot. That's how we get a better understanding of which tasks align with the season we're in and which ones can be deferred. Likewise, reflecting on the results of our work also gives us insight. If we've been investing time and energy in something that doesn't seem to be taking root, it could be that our timing is off. That's when it might be to our benefit to lay it down for a while and pick it back up later when circumstances have changed.

Spending time in prayer to figure out where we are in any phase of our lives clarifies not only what we can accomplish but what we can expect. Having realistic expectations of ourselves and of others in the season we're in gives us the upper hand in the battle against tension.

Bloom and Flourish

My mom has a beautiful maple tree in her side yard. When she placed a bench beneath it, my siblings and I decided to landscape the shady space around it as a gift for Mother's Day. Off I went to the nursery with the money the seven of us had chipped in. I knew enough to seek out flowers of different heights, colors, and textures. I also knew enough to look at the tags to see what would thrive in the shade of the tree. However, the flowers that grow in full sun were far prettier and more vibrant than those that grow in the shade. So, me being me, I ignored the full-sun icon on the tags and bought all the wrong plants, simply because I wanted them — as if my sheer determination and will could alter nature itself.

That first week, the space looked fantastic! The plants were healthy, and the colors were spectacular. Sadly, it was all downhill from there, as every single flower wilted and died from the lack of sun. After wasting all that time and money, I learned to accept that the flowers that grow best in that shady space are impatiens. How ironic: It was my own impatience that led me to buy the wrong flowers in the first place!

Although we try our best to control what will grow in our lives and when, there's no such thing as a special-order life. God is in charge. Fortunately for us, he's not a cheap-flower-of-the-moment guy. Never restricted by a budget, he spends his love freely and lavishly, planting seeds within us that he's chosen specifically for each one of us, seeds that have the most exquisite potential, if we nurture them.

It's by honoring his timing in our lives that we grow our roots deep into the soil of his will.

The way to cultivate those seeds is to embrace the seasons he's laid out for us. It's by honoring his timing in our lives that we grow our roots deep into the soil of his will. When we take up what we're meant to do in the moment, and lay down for a while what we aren't, we find we have the energy we need for the journey. Suddenly, there's time and space to enjoy what's before us. Moreover, stress and tension wither and die because they're denied what they need to thrive. As we soak up God's grace and will for us, we bloom in the most spectacular ways.

••

At His Feet

Magnificent Gardener,

Water my faith so my roots will grow deep into your will. Grant me the wisdom to discern what you're asking of me now and what can be deferred to another time. Partner with me to starve tension and stress of what they need to grow by aligning my expectations of myself and others with the season we're in.

Should I be in a time seemingly void of your blessings, help me understand that you may be asking me to rest. My remaining fallow for a time will allow you to revitalize me with what I need for the beauty to come. When the small green shoots of the purpose you've planted within me finally break through, bless me with the patience I need to honor your timing for when to take action. Increase my trust in the fact that whatever you've started in me you will bring to fruition. When I do reap a bountiful harvest, prompt me to share those blessings with others. It's by spreading your warmth, and watering others with your grace, that I help grow what lies dormant in them.

I ask this in Jesus' name. Amen.

Unwrapping the G-I-F-T

Gauge — How would I define this season of my life? Are there any tasks or expectations I have that don't align with this season? What emotions are they causing me?

Invite — What happens when I invite those feelings in and sit with them at God's feet?

Filter — What do I see when I look at the situation through the filter of God's loving eyes?

Transform — Are there any tasks God is counseling me to lay down for a while? What expectations of myself and others do I need to let go of for now? What are some concrete steps I can take to do so?

6
Preventing Comparison

Lord, do you not care that my sister has
left me to do all the work by myself?
— Luke 10:40

Back to the barbed-wire fences in chapter 3. They may not have served well for personal boundaries, but they sure did make handy laundry lines. There were no washing machines or dryers in the remote village where I did missionary work. We spent our Saturdays washing our clothes by hand and putting them outside to dry on the fence. The good news is, prickly wire catches fabric right away, eliminating any need for clothespins. The bad news is, prickly wire shreds fabric when you quickly pull it off. Every time I did laundry, the sky would be clear, with the sun shining bright. I always forgot about the region's fast-rolling storms. Inevitably, one would appear out of nowhere, soaking my clothes faster than I could pull them off the line. With each item I ripped off the fence, another hole was ripped in my clothes. I'm nowhere close to being a saint, but I did end up with an entire wardrobe of holey clothes.

As you can imagine, those clothes eventually gave out with all those rips and tears. By the end of my first year in mission, I had no choice but to toss them and shop for more. My annual stipend was $600 a year — not enough to invest in a new wardrobe. I did have a wonderful Guatemalan co-worker, though, who knew just what to do. Albertina took me by the hand and led the way.

Several chicken-bus rides later, we were in Guatemala City in a thrift store. Unlike our clean, organized secondhand stores in the States, this one had absolutely no rhyme or reason to it. Nothing was on a hanger. Nothing was categorized by size. It wasn't even clear where the line was drawn between kids' clothes and adults'. The second-, third-, and sometimes fourth-hand clothes were just stacked in piles, willy-nilly, everywhere.

Albertina went right to work, rolling up her sleeves and digging in. When she presented me with her findings, I noticed that the sizes on the tags were all rubbed off, and there were no dressing rooms or mirrors in sight. When I asked where I could try everything on, she just laughed. She proceeded to size the clothes for me. For the shirts and dresses, she held them up to me and judged with her eyes. For the pants, she folded the waist in half and wrapped it around my neck. If they didn't choke me, she declared, they'd fit around my waist. Who knew that the circumference of the average person's neck is half the size of her waist?

When I got back to my house, I tried on the clothes. Yes, they fit, but there wasn't a single item that flattered me. In fact, it was the exact opposite: Almost every item emphasized my flaws. I'm short-waisted with a pale complexion. Had I been able to try on the clothes and look in a mirror, I would have realized they were all made for someone with a longer torso and darker complexion.

I looked short, chubby, washed out, and sallow. The dreadful combination made me self-conscious and insecure. It only got worse each time I caught a glimpse of myself in a mirror or a window. I was reminded all over again of my shortcomings, triggering my envy of women taller and darker than me.

Much to my chagrin, there were no such things as sales receipts or return policies. I'd blown what little money I had and was stuck with the clothes I'd bought. I had to keep reminding myself that they were functional. Besides, I was there to help others, not to win a fashion contest. So I stopped comparing how I wanted to look with how I *did* look, and wore the clothes for the entire year to come.

Competing and Comparing

Comparison definitely enters the picture during the dinner party in Luke 10. When Mary chooses to sit at Jesus' feet while Martha chooses to serve, I think initially Jesus approves. He knows both decisions are made with the sisters' hearts. Each sister is living out her "better part" by drawing closer to God with her choice. It's clear that sitting and listening to all that Jesus has to say definitely brings Mary closer to God. After all, Jesus affirms her choice by calling it "the better part." Yet choosing to serve Jesus as Martha does can bring her closer to God too. There's a sacrifice that comes from serving and a beauty in putting others' needs before our own. Both paths lead straight to God. Martha's problem isn't that she chooses to serve. It's that she eventually compares her choice with her sister's.

The more Martha focuses on competing with Mary in her heart, the less room there is to serve with it.

The moment Martha begins to compare Mary's choice with her own is the exact moment Martha stops serving with her heart. It's also the moment she begins a competition in her mind, one she's bound and determined to win. The more Martha focuses on competing with Mary in her heart, the less room there is to serve with it. That's why every task from that moment forward fills Martha with tension rather than joy. It's also what drives her to Jesus with a question phrased to make him compare her efforts with her sister's. She wants him to be the one to declare her the winner of her imagined competition, never realizing she's clothing herself with the wrong intention. Had there been a mirror nearby, and had Martha slowed down long enough to look into it, she would have seen how poorly that intention fit her.

Martha has the opportunity of a lifetime by having Jesus in her very own living room. Her initial choice of serving him with her whole heart looks absolutely stunning on her! It highlights all her best features, complimenting her in all the ways she's been blessed. Hosting is what she was born to do. And I believe that when Martha gives her all while serving, she feels a deep peace and purpose in being the woman God is calling her to be. She knows that hospitality matters. It's a ministry all its own. Making people feel welcomed and honored fills them with dignity, affirming their self-worth. Sadly, Martha loses sight of her own self-worth when she starts envying Mary's choice more than valuing her own.

Why do we do this? Why are we quite content with our choices until we look at the ones others are making? Why are we perfectly happy with the direction of our lives until we see where others are headed? Whenever we look to others for affirmation, we end up comparing ourselves with them. Pile on a need to compete against those we feel challenged by, and peace flies out the window, allowing stress to come in through the door. And when we think we've won this imagined competition, we feel a false sense of self-worth. And when we lose? Oh, my! The list of stress-filled words that envelop us has no end. It's like trying on someone else's clothes that are three sizes too big or too small. We're never going to look good when we look in the mirror. Worse yet, like a tabloid magazine with two women in the same outfit being rated for "Who wore it best?" we see a big, fat 0 stamped on ourselves.

The rating system goes on as we tally up all the ways we fall short and all the ways others have it better. As crazy as it sounds, this behavior becomes addictive. It's easier to label ourselves victims than it is to change where we're looking or make the needed changes in ourselves. So we continue looking outward at others; wanting what they have, coveting what they do, and envying who they are. We reach a point at which we can't take our eyes off whatever piques our interest, even if it distresses our souls.

There's no more dangerous place for this than social media. It's an immense thrill to be a fly on the wall of other people's lives. It feeds our curiosity and captivates our minds. Without meaning to, we scroll down the slippery slope and can't seem to stop. And as overindulging in anything leaves us sluggish, bloated, and uncomfortable, viewing the glossy moments of other people's lives demotivates us, slowing us down. It also prevents us from doing what we're supposed to be doing in our own lives. As Glynnis Whitwer says in her book *Taming the To-Do List: How to Choose Your Best Work Every Day*: "What better way to limit the power of God's kingdom than by getting God's followers to not do what they know they should?"* Worse yet, binging on anything that makes us feel like less, be it online or in person, bloats the victim side of us, making it feel as if our own lives don't fit anymore.

This is when the Martha side of us starts creating our battle plan with God. We accuse him of not caring that we don't have enough; we never consider that the problem is our caring too

---

*Glynnis Whitwer, *Taming the To-Do List: How to Choose Your Best Work Every Day* (Grand Rapids, MI: Revell, 2015), 33.

much about what others have. Rather than looking to God for guidance on how to get ourselves out of this awful spiral, we strategize all the ways we want him to change our circumstances so we can have what we see all around us. The thing is, that's a hunger that's insatiable. Someone is always going to have it better than we do. Someone is always going to look better than we do.

We accuse him of not caring that we don't have enough; we never consider that the problem is our caring too much about what others have.

As Martha learns, God will never feed our bulimic side. His love is a healthy diet of acceptance of exactly who we are, combined with a vision of who he's created us to be. Our exercise plan is to do whatever it takes to get us there. Ask any of the "couch potatoes" my husband has taught and trained to run a 5K: It's always a challenge in the beginning. But when those people cross the finish line of their first race, they feel like a million bucks. They certainly don't become Olympic athletes, but the Couch to 5K program teaches them that success comes with moderation in everything.

Sadly, there are very few of us who use moderation when surfing social media. According to Maryam Mohsin in her article "10 Social Media Statistics You Need to Know in 2020," the average person spends three hours a day on social media and messaging.* We may plan on logging on for "just five minutes" to catch up on what we've missed, but we climb out of the rabbit hole hours later, wondering where the time

---

*Maryam Mohsin, "10 Social Media Statistics You Need to Know in 2020," Oberlo.com, August 7, 2020, https://www.oberlo.com/blog/social-media-marketing-statistics.

went. Not only have we lost time we never intended to waste, but we often feel worse about ourselves than we did before we logged on. All those glossy photos have us convinced that we're the only ones not living a perfect life.

Obviously, there were no cell phones or social media in Martha's day. Based on what we know about her personality, though, there's a strong chance that she would have fallen down the rabbit hole too. On social media she would have found more great ideas for entertaining, but she would have fallen prey to envy when she noticed that the pictures of her dinner party didn't match up to the posts on other people's feeds. Worse yet, instead of going to Jesus with her tension, she may have gone to her girlfriends, texting them routinely about her growing frustration with her sister. Of course, sharing our situation with family and friends helps us feel heard. But if we use their sympathy to justify our fury, it becomes fuel for tension's fire. It's only by looking in the right direction, upward to God, that we're guaranteed a true balm for our souls. He's the one who fills us with peace and appreciation for exactly who we are. In fact, when we look to him, we become radiant (see Ps 34:5).

Preventing Comparison

Along with offering us the true balm for our souls and making us radiant, God gives us free will. We aren't meant to be controlled by anyone or anything. Toward that end, we need to reflect on when and where we feel comparison controlling us. Does it happen while we're on social media? Are there certain social situations in which we feel less than others? Are there other areas or times that trigger our need to compare or compete? Identifying the scenarios that make us vulnerable is the first step in the process.

The second step is getting honest about our time spent in the comparison game. If we truly want to address the issue and make a change, we need to know the entire reality of our situation. Tallying the time spent on jealous thoughts can be helpful, just as counting calories can be for a dieter. Whether we quickly note the moments in a journal or draw tally marks while scrolling through our phones, we can concretely see just how often our thoughts are taken captive by comparison and envy. None of this should be done with the intention of feeling bad about ourselves. It should be done to understand the truth about our habits. Even if we're only surfing for short bits here and there or fixating now and again on what others have, we're likely to be astounded by the grand total of time spent on jealous thoughts each day.

Once we understand just how vulnerable we are, we have to shift our gaze to where it's supposed to be. Lifting our eyes to God allows us to see the way he does. We can't do that if our heads are constantly down, focused on our phones. Nor can we look to him if we're too busy looking at others, envying what they have, or comparing our choices with theirs, as Martha does. When we unplug from our envious thoughts and routinely plug in to God, he reminds us who we are and whose we are. Each of us is fearfully and wonderfully made (see Ps 139:14) by the one, true, sovereign God. He made us perfectly in his image, and we will always be his cherished children. Our ever-loving Father delights in us always, exactly as we are. Once we're reminded of this, why would we need to compare ourselves with anyone ever again?

When we go to God for healing in the comparison game, he doesn't merely heal us. He also highlights all the good in our lives, along with the individual gifts and talents he's blessed us with. When we look at ourselves in the mirror of his unconditional love, we see the beauty of those gifts reflected back at us, and our self-worth is reaffirmed. Moreover, by keeping our eyes on God, we see there's no longer a reason to compete or compare because we know in our hearts that he sees us doing our best. Even when things get challenging, we recognize "he who fashions the hearts of them all, / and observes all their deeds" (Ps 33:15). Being seen by him, being loved by him through our efforts, makes it all worth it. We feel valued. We feel peace.

A Tailor-Made Life

During my second year in Guatemala, a friend discovered an amazing seamstress. This humble Guatemalan woman never used sewing patterns. Remarkably, she could create whatever you described or duplicate any item you brought her way. Regardless of what she made, she always created it to fit each customer perfectly. When I saw the fantastic work she produced, I started saving my money. Fortunately, she didn't charge much. By my third year there, I had a tailor-made wardrobe unique to me. The tops and skirts were simple, but each garment was one of a kind, and I wore them proudly.

God made us in his image, with a tailor-made life unique to each of us. When we attempt to put someone else's life on, not only does it not suit us, but it leaves the beautiful life we're supposed to live discarded, like a cast-off garment on our closet floor. Rather, we need to clothe ourselves with the unique strengths and gifts God has given us. When we do, and we see how stunning we look in the mirror of his unconditional love, we'll never have to compete or compare again. Remaining confidently robed in his love, we'll live out our own better part, and our beauty will be enhanced because of it.

••

At His Feet

Sovereign Designer of All,

Inspire me to see myself through your eyes: perfectly made and unconditionally loved. Remind me of this when I begin to falter, comparing myself with others, competing against them for their approval and affirmation. Place mirrors all around me to reflect that no one else's life but my own will ever suit me for who you created me to be.

When I become vulnerable to comparison in certain situations or while on social media, help me to recognize when my mind is taken captive by jealous thoughts. Then, most of all, remind me to unplug from what distresses me and plug into you so I discover the tailor-made life you've designed specifically for me. Help me to dress myself in it so I may live out my gifts and talents, radiating the light and beauty you've placed within me. Prompt me to look to you always so I make all my choices with right intention, adorning myself with your grace at all times.

I ask this in Jesus' name. Amen.

——————————————

Unwrapping the G-I-F-T

Gauge — Do I compare myself and my choices to others and their choices? What emotions do I feel when I'm scrolling through social media? Are there certain social situations in which I become vulnerable to comparison? If so, how does that make me feel?

Invite — What happens when I invite those feelings in and sit with them at God's feet?

Filter — What do I see when I look at the situation through the filter of God's loving eyes?

Transform — What safeguards can I put in place to prevent me from comparing myself to others? How can I go about clothing myself with the life God has tailor-made for me?

7
Asking for Help

Tell her then to help me.
— Luke 10:40

I've never been a Candy Land or Chutes and Ladders kind of mom. Those slow-moving board games are more torturous for me than watching paint dry. I'm more the imaginative, hands-on type, and I especially love activities that produce an end result (a Martha trait, I'm sure). As soon as my kids were old enough to resist putting small objects in their mouths, I introduced them to LEGOs. Initially, each of my kids allowed me to teach them every aspect of putting together a boxed set. They'd patiently listen as I explained the general concepts that go into building. They'd attentively look on as I demonstrated, step by step, how to connect the bricks so they looked like the pictures in the instruction booklet. The minute things began to click to-gether in their minds, however, each of them would inevitably proclaim, "I want to do it all by myself!" I'd try to convince them we should work as a team, but the independence gene runs deep in the McGarry family. Inevitably, I'd get demoted from teacher to instruction-book page turner, forced to passively sit by at our kiddie table as they built without me.

Usually, I was okay with that because, in my mind, I was making myself ready and available to help them when they needed it. In their minds, however, I was just an audience mem-ber being entertained and amazed by their ability. Even when they hit a snag they couldn't overcome, they'd deflect any offer of assistance I made. Instead, they'd scrunch up their little faces in deep concentration, convinced they could figure it out if they just tried harder. The more intricate the steps, the more their frustration grew. Even though I was right there beside them, constantly offering to help, they kept repeating the same refrain: "I want to do it all by myself!"

As a Martha with my own control issues, it was painful not to be allowed to help, especially when I knew a temper tantrum was brewing. From my perspective, the resolution to the prob-lem was so easy and clear. But no matter how I phrased my offer to help, they always responded with that same darn reply: "I want to do it all by myself!"

Being a Martyr

I think Martha is someone who wants to do things all by her-self. She understands the concept behind constructing a dinner party. She also knows all the parts that need to come together to make it happen. In her extravagant love for Jesus, she's laid out additional pieces to be added to take this meal to an en-tirely new level. She wants to build a masterpiece worthy of her Master. And why not? She's been blessed with a lot of energy and a strong work ethic. She's certain that if she just leans on both, she'll get the job done. But the more intricate things get, the more things don't seem to click together. As her tension rises, she becomes more and more off-kilter. No matter how askew things get, though, she still won't ask her sister for help.

We're never told why Martha doesn't come right out and ask Mary for assistance. Maybe, like my kids, Martha's independence gene runs deep. Perhaps, like me, she has a high need for control, making her think that if she does it all by herself, she's guaranteed that things will be assembled her way. Perhaps she doesn't work well with others and prefers an audience to a partner. No matter her reason, she's learning the hard way that building anything is difficult, especially if there are no coffee breaks and no teamwork. Consequently, Martha's foundation is cracking underneath her with the weight of work enough for two.

If she does it all by herself, she's guaranteed that things will be assembled her way.

There are always two sides to every story, though. We have to wonder why Mary doesn't get up and offer to help. Even culturally, where every woman in their day was accustomed to doing kitchen work, it just doesn't make sense. Mary sits and listens to every word Jesus says. If she lives out his message, loving her neighbor as herself, wouldn't that include her sister and offering to help her? Although we'll never know, it doesn't stop me from wondering if maybe Mary had offered to help, again and again, all through the years, at every dinner party since she and Martha became responsible for the household. But Martha took such great pride in how she entertained her guests, she kept deflecting the help. Maybe, eventually, Mary stopped offering because she knew she'd be rejected. Why would this time be any different?

Whatever her motive, when Mary doesn't offer to help, Martha stacks her frustration higher and higher. With every new level Martha clicks on top, the tower teeters more and more. Inevitably, it comes crashing down. Like a child who heads straight to a parent when a sibling knocks down a LEGO creation, Martha bypasses her sister and goes straight to Jesus. She demands that he tell Martha to help.

There are so many reasons why a lot of us Marthas don't ask for help: We're too proud to admit we can't do it all alone. We're too controlling and want things done our way. We're too meek and don't want to inconvenience anyone. We're convinced it's all part of our job description as women, and we feel inept if we can't pull it off. The list of reasons is endless.

No matter our reason, when we don't ask for help, our tension mounts gradually. Often, we don't even realize we've added too many additional pieces to what we're constructing until our stress level spikes. As fate would have it, it's always during the most inopportune times: when company is over, when time is of the essence and won't allow for us to reconfigure things, when the tower is teetering and it's critical we keep it from crashing down. So we push on through, assembling whatever's required of us in the moment, planning to address the imbalance later. When later finally comes, our stress level isn't as high, and we wonder what we were making such a big fuss about. It's so much easier to continue on with things as they are than to invest the time and energy it would take to reconstruct how things should be in our lives. That's when we can learn from the wisdom of those who came before us, those who lived through our same syndrome of trying to hold things all together, while bearing up under the weight alone.

Asking for Help

Moses was guilty of trying to do it all by himself after he led his people out of Egypt. As they wandered in the wilderness, the Israelites had a plethora of opinions among them. Disagreements inevitably broke out, and they needed someone to settle their disputes. There were more than two million people, so we can only imagine how many disputes there were. At first, Moses tried to handle it all himself. It took the wisdom of his father-in-law, Jethro, to help him see that going it alone wasn't good. "When Moses' father-in-law saw all that he was doing for the people, he said, 'What is this that you are doing for the people? Why do you sit alone, while all the people stand around you from morning until evening? … What you are doing is not good. You will surely wear yourself out, both you and these people with you. For the task is too heavy for you; you cannot do it alone" (Ex 18:14, 17–18).

Jethro knew that it's never advisable to build any structure on a single pillar of support. Moses was going to topple from all the exertion. What good would he be to his people then? Jethro outlined exactly how Moses should "look for able men among all the people, men who fear God, are trustworthy, and hate dishonest gain; set such men over them as officers over thousands, hundreds, fifties and tens" (Ex 18:21). The people Moses appointed could judge the minor cases and bring only the difficult ones to him. Moses recognized a good idea when he heard one and immediately implemented the advice.

Despite being divine, Jesus needed help too. As a carpenter, he knew a thing or two about building. If you want something to last, the construction has to be well thought out and include plenty of supports to carry the weight. He applied the same concepts when building God's kingdom here on earth. He couldn't risk being a Moses, having it all lean on him, only to fall to pieces when it came time to go. The Gospel of Luke says, "Now during those days he went out to the mountain to pray; and he spent the night in prayer to God. And when day came, he called his disciples and chose twelve of them, whom he also named apostles" (Lk 6:12–13). By asking others for help, Jesus knew he'd be empowering them to bless the world with their gifts and talents. Moreover, if he trusted the apostles with responsibility, they'd not only help him carry out his work while he was with them, they'd carry it on after he was gone. As was his way, Jesus never made these decisions lightly or on his own. He always went to his Father for guidance. By going up the mountain to pray, Jesus sought God's counsel in choosing which twelve pillars would best uphold the kingdom to be built.

By asking others for help, Jesus knew he'd be empowering them to bless the world with their gifts and talents.

We should follow Moses and Jesus' examples in whatever we're building, be it a family, a business, or a ministry. It's logical to create and carry out a master plan when doing so. I've already talked about trimming back the extras and deferring what can be done to a later time. Now, after defining what really needs to be done, we should "go up the mountain to pray," seeking God's advice to determine who can help and with what, to distribute the weight evenly. That's how we cut down tension's ability to shake our foundations. That's how we prevent things from crashing down around us.

As we spend time with God, he'll remind us of the tasks that *only we* can do. From there, it's easy to see what can be done by others. Based on the people around us and their unique talents and potential, God will help us see the best individuals suited to each task. As difficult as it may be, we will then have to humble ourselves and graciously ask them for help, knowing we're offering them an opportunity for growth and a chance to be part of something bigger.

Redistributing the Weight

When my kids were eight, twelve, and fourteen, I went back to work. Despite spending my days at the office, I spent all my early mornings and evenings trying to carry out all the at-home tasks I'd been doing for years. Slowly but surely, I began to fall apart. In the process, I was turning into someone I no longer liked, screaming and yelling as a way to release the compounding stress. When everything finally came crashing down, I found myself at God's feet, demanding, like Martha, that he tell everyone in my world to get up and help. Instead, he inspired me to use the G-I-F-T method to dig my way out of the rubble. I will never stop being amazed at what God reveals to me when I turn to him. Equipped with his solution, I called a family meeting.

As my husband and kids sat on the couch, I gathered some LEGOs. It wasn't lost on me that in order to get the bricks I needed, I had to disassemble some of the previous structures we'd built before. Then I placed five stacks of bricks on the ottoman in front of my husband and kids, one stack for each of us. I explained that the individual bricks represented what each of us was currently responsible for in the household. The visual of their small stacks next to my skyscraper sent the message loud and clear: Our world was leaning off-kilter because of the imbalance. Knowing it's human nature to take more ownership when we volunteer for something (versus being told to do it), I asked my little family which tasks of mine they could take on. I was blown away by their sincere desire to help. With each offer they made, I took a brick from my stack and clicked it onto theirs. After just five minutes, the tasks were almost evenly distributed, and it was done with right intention.

I won't claim it's been smooth sailing ever since. There have certainly been tremors of frustration that have shaken our world when my kids haven't followed through on what they promised. They're still kids, after all. But the initial goal of lightening my load has been met, and I'm no longer at risk for collapse. The additional blessing is that, with every chore my kids carry out, I see new growth and strength in them. Little by little, they're becoming people I can lean on. I don't plan on confusing our roles, thinking things should always be even; I'm still the parent, and they're still the kids. But the more they carry out their responsibilities, the more we click together as a family. I'm also watching them mature right before my very eyes, becoming the people God created them to be.

God gifts each of us with the different pieces we need to build our lives. We just need to turn to him and receive them. As part of his master plan, he purposefully and carefully gives each of us different gifts so we're forced to work together. He has no interest in a kingdom built by one. That's too much weight for anyone to bear, and it stunts the growth of everyone else. God wants us to turn to him and to others for help. Each time we do, we build community, connecting our lives in meaningful ways. That progression of teamwork naturally builds us all up, moving us forward, keeping us perfectly aligned to live out the better part.

••

At His Feet

Master Builder,

I want to do what I can to build your kingdom here on earth. Sometimes, though, I want that so much that I take on more than I should, and I feel the weight of it all on my shoulders. Before I begin to crumble, help me recognize that you never intended for me to carry it all alone. Humble me to see this need for help as a gift: It's your reminder that I need to turn to you for counsel and support and need to turn to others for their assistance.

Before I ask for help, prevent me from demanding it in anger or frustration. Give me the strength and insight I need to become vulnerable, asking with grace, to inspire others to step up, with right intention, to take ownership of their part. Above all, help me realize that by distributing the weight of responsibility, I'm empowering others to grow and contribute their gifts and talents. That's what strengthens the foundation of community, creating a level surface for you to build upon.

I ask this in Jesus' name. Amen.

Unwrapping the G-I-F-T

Gauge — In what areas of my life do I feel the weight of work enough for two resting all on my shoulders? How does it feel to try to hold that up all by myself?

Invite — What happens when I invite those feelings in and sit with them at God's feet?

Filter — What do I see when I look at the situation through the filter of God's loving eyes?

Transform — Which tasks can I ask others to help with? Who is best suited to each one? How do I go about asking so they feel empowered and willing to help?

8
Defining Priorities

But the Lord answered her, "Martha, Martha, you
are worried and distracted by many things."
— Luke 10:41

Until a few years ago, I had an old metallic-blue, slide-out cell phone with a keyboard. I *loved* that thing! Of course, everyone around me found it hilarious. They were already sporting iPhones and thought I was living in the dinosaur age. I didn't care. Whenever I slid that hidden keyboard out, I felt like a secret agent. Plus, I'm a writer. I loved the lettered keys I could press like those on a typewriter. I had no interest in a touchscreen.

But when you want to advance your writing career and build a "platform," you have to go with the technology that supports that. I wasn't able to snap pictures on "Old Blue" and easily upload them to Instagram or Facebook. Trying to stayed focused on my objective, the sad day came when I had to retire my old-school phone and get an iPhone 6S. Once again, I thought I was "all that" and cutting edge. Once again, everyone laughed at me because, by then, they all had iPhone 9s and 10s. My friend Pam one-upped us all and got the new iPhone 11. That thing can do just about everything but wash and fold your laundry! It can charge other people's phones just by coming into contact with them and can survive being submerged in a pool for up to thirty minutes. Moreover, it doesn't just have one camera, but three!

The catch is: Whenever Pam takes a picture of our friend Jess and me, I never know which camera lens to look at. In every photo she's taken of us, I'm smiling big, but I'm never looking in the right direction. I keep trying the process of elimination, figuring eventually I'll choose the right lens to look at.

Getting Distracted

When Martha greets Jesus at the door, she's focused on her objective. She wants to serve him with her whole heart, and that desire is fixed and firm. Additionally, she has a clear picture in her mind of how that will look. As she gets absorbed by her many tasks, though, she finds her sight wandering, distracted by every out-of-place item and yet-to-be-done chore. In no time at all, she loses focus and is completely confused as to where to look. She tries the process of elimination, and every other trick she can think of, to find her way back to her initial perspective. But there are too many distractions, too many shiny objects catching her eye, too many thoughts and ideas swirling around in her mind.

As things get blurry, she loses sight of where to place her heart. In her unfocused state, she forgets that this dinner party is about capturing a moment in time spent with Jesus. Instead, she fixates on enhancing the backdrop, as if for a photo she'll frame for her wall. This new priority inspires her to double her efforts, distracting her even more from her initial intention. The irony is, she doesn't become distracted from her work; she gets distracted *by* it. Vulnerable to her desire to do more, rather than less, she convinces herself that all the things she *wants* to do now *need* to be done. The more she gets distracted by her work, the more her tension rises. The more her tension rises, the more it becomes her focus. Whenever we give tension the spotlight, it always steals the show. It also morphs and takes on the multiple roles of frustration, stress, and, worst of all, worry. Worry, like any emotion rooted in fear, is

Worry, like any emotion rooted in fear, is like an out-of-focus camera: It robs even the beautiful moments of light and clarity.

like an out-of-focus camera: It robs even the beautiful moments of light and clarity. While distraction derails our efforts to get things done, worry causes our tension to spike. I believe that when worry enters the picture and tells Martha she won't get it all done in time, her tension doesn't just spike; it skyrockets.

Worry is every Martha's Achilles heel. As Proverbs 12:25 says, "Anxiety weighs down the human heart." Worry penetrates our armor of elaborate planning and advance preparations, disabling us, leaving us limping. Despite being extremely focused and accomplishing so much when our priorities are clear, the moment we allow worry to enter the picture, it's like putting on the wrong camera filter: Everything gets blurry. The more our efforts get derailed, the more our angst rises. It's the worst feeling in the world when we realize we won't be able to follow through on what we've promised, whether it's to someone else or to ourselves.

When worry partners with distraction, they become a dynamic duo that's hard to beat. One lobs the ball to the other, and the other hits it back. Back and forth, worry and distraction feed and engorge each other. Like a ball in a tennis match, we get caught in the volley, with tension batting us around and beating us down. Unlike tennis, there is no love in this match. Instead, the two push right intention and love out of view. That's when we need to turn to the origin of love himself to end this terrible cycle and provide the clarity we need.

Defining Priorities

Thankfully, Jesus always does both — ends the terrible cycle and provides clarity — regardless of the strength of our tension or our approach. For her part, Martha approaches him with guns blazing. She holds nothing back when she spews her tension all over him. Most people would be inclined either to fire back when approached like this or to turn on their heels and walk away. But not Jesus. He answers Martha. As he does for every prayer ever uttered, Jesus listens and he responds. He may not give us the answers we're looking for, but he'll always give us the answers that are best for us.

Sure enough, that's what he does with Martha. Knowing he needs to deliver a tough-love message to inspire her to refocus her efforts, he softens his opening statement by repeating her name twice as a sign of intimacy, as a loving endearment. He knows her wholly and completely, inside and out, just as he knows each one of us. He can see what she lacks and what she longs for. He knows that his Father is the answer to both. To lead her to him, Jesus needs her to listen to his every word. With that goal in mind, he says her name the first time to prick up her hearing so he can speak directly into her ears. He then says her name a second time to lift up her eyes so he can speak directly into her heart.

Once her sight is refocused on him, he shows her the snapshot from his point of view. She goes to Jesus looking to get help for her many tasks. What she isn't expecting is that he'll give her new eyes to see the one task that really needs to be done. With a perspective that is always a holy one, he wants to teach her how to look at things through his lens. He knows that once she does, her right priorities will crystallize, her stress will dissolve, and everything will be picture-perfect from that new angle.

Jesus is the perfect one to teach us how to view our lives. Whereas the new iPhone has multiple filters to look through, Jesus reveals that the only one worth looking through is "the better part." When we apply the filter of wanting to draw closer to God, we clearly see what tasks in our day, done with the right intentions, will lead to that end. Keeping that filter in place will ensure that we stay focused, allowing what isn't necessary to fade into the background. The crazy thing is that accomplishing things from this godly perspective doesn't drain us, regardless of how much there is to do. In fact, we're rejuvenated because we're drawn closer to the Source of energy himself. One cell phone's recharging another one when they connect is a new concept in the tech world, but God's rejuvenating us when we reconnect with him is as old as time.

We're rejuvenated because we're drawn closer to the Source of energy himself.

Not only is God an energy restorer, he's a mathematician and miracle maker. As Kristin Armstrong says in her book *Heart of My Heart: 365 Reflections on the Magnitude and Meaning of*

Motherhood, God can do with us what he did with the loaves and the fishes: "I ask him to take what I have to offer and bless it as he blessed the loaves and fishes, making enough of me to go around. That prayer has made a difference every single time. He either expands time or amplifies me. Whatever it is, it works. Suddenly I can go about my regular tasks and I don't run empty."* Armstrong goes on to explain that just as the disciples were able to fill twelve baskets with the leftovers from that miracle long ago, we find leftover energy for ourselves, despite having given our all to whatever tasks we've accomplished.

The more we practice going to God for his perspective, the more we feel the benefits. Our renewed energy and clearer focus have us looking at things completely differently. Before we know it, we're swapping out our almighty list for the Almighty's list. In place of writing a to-do list, we find ourselves writing a to-whom list, with every task, no matter how mundane, being carried out as an offering to him.

No longer using a wide-angle lens that automatically zooms in on every shiny object and distraction, we don't get sidetracked and pulled in different directions anymore. The feeling that we're just chasing our tails, running around putting out fires, is gone. Moreover, where our old vulnerability had us dancing to the demands of others, letting their agendas dictate ours, now we look to God to determine what really needs to be done. That's how we shift from being people pleasers to being God pleasers.

God has already preordained what each one of us should do in our lives. If we go to him, he'll make sure that when we're busy, we're busy doing the right things, with the right intentions. And no matter how busy that can get, if we put on the armor of God, our Achilles heel will be shielded from the poisoned arrows of worry and other fear-based emotions. Those arrows will no

---

*Kristin Armstrong, *Heart of My Heart: 365 Reflections on the Magnitude and Meaning of Motherhood* (New York: FaithWords, 2010), 88.

longer hit their mark. Our godly perspective will keep our focus clear, our battery charged at all times, and all distractions out of the picture.

The first step toward achieving that is seeing things from God's perspective. Just as we may need to move to a different spot to get a strong cell phone signal, we may need to experiment a bit with where we get the strongest connection with God. Find a quiet place. Create a prayer space there with a comfortable place to sit or kneel, adding visual prompts to keep you focused on God. The effects of returning to the same space and spending time there with God are astounding! Just as repeating certain physical exercises teaches our bodies muscle memory, returning to the same spot in our prayer time teaches our souls spiritual memory. The more we do it, the stronger and faster the connection with God gets.

Once connected, simply asking "How do you want me to serve you today?" starts the process of letting God define his priorities for us. Keep in mind that everything we do for others, with right intention, we do for him. When distracting thoughts and ideas enter the picture, imagining his response to the question "Will this draw me closer to you?" will clarify what we should act on and what we should set aside. Asking God to bless each item on our list helps us prioritize and carry it out. And when tension rears its ugly head, returning to God for his perspective and asking for a multiplication miracle tend to do the trick.

A Different View

Completely confused as to why the iPhone 11 has three cameras, I did some research. The more I read, the more it seemed they were describing the Trinity. Like God the Father, God the Son, and God the Holy Spirit, the three cameras in an iPhone 11 work together, switching between one another, quickly and seamlessly, to create the best picture possible. Combining information and perspective, they blur out the background and zoom in on the focal point. They also provide better depth-control, compensate for low light, and, despite distance, still produce a stunning image.

That's what the Holy Trinity does for us. When we go to them for their perspective, they clarify what our focal points should be. They also guide us in how to make distractions, worry, and all negative emotions rooted in fear blur into the background. It's with their help that we're able to zoom in on what really matters, maintain the energy we need to carry it out, and resist any distractions that try to derail us on the way. The end result is that our lives become stunning images in the photo album of God's love.

• •

At His Feet

Marvelous Seer of All,

When I'm bombarded with distractions and worry that blur my vision and drain my energy, remind me to turn to you. Rather than trying to escape my reality, prompt me to create a sacred space where I can be with you. As I routinely connect with you there, refocus my perspective so it aligns with yours, illuminating all the ways you want me to serve you and others. Recharge my soul so I will have what I need to carry that out. Reinforce all the ways I'm susceptible to the distractions and shiny objects of this world. Deflect the arrows of worry with the armor of your love.

Grant me a multiplication miracle so I will have leftover energy to enjoy the good things you've blessed me with. I know that you capture the events of my life in your heart, like snapshots. But the ones that bring you the most joy are the ones in which I am smiling big, with my eyes focused directly on you.

I ask this in Jesus' name. Amen.

Unwrapping the G-I-F-T

Gauge — When am I most susceptible to distractions and worry? How do I typically respond? What emotions result from my response?

Invite — What happens when I invite those feelings in and sit with them at God's feet?

Filter — What do I see when I look at the situation through the filter of God's loving eyes?

Transform — How can I routinely return to God for his perspective? What can I do to keep distractions and worry at bay?

9
Valuing Self-Care

There is need of only one thing.
— Luke 10:42

Shortly after I graduated from college, a friend gave me a horse. I made the choice to live at home so I could afford to board it at a fancy barn half an hour away. Despite the distance, I visited the barn as often as I could.

One day, I stayed later than usual and ended up driving home in the dark. As the red light glowed on the dashboard of my car, telling me I was close to running out of gas, I was too tired and lazy to heed the warning. I was at that age when I thought I knew it all and could defy reality with my optimism. The moment my car wouldn't accelerate when I stepped on the gas was a rude awakening for me. Ignoring the signs and powering through doesn't change reality. When we're running on fumes and don't stop to refuel, we'll inevitably run out of gas. Fortunately, I was traveling fast enough to pull over to the far right and coast halfway down the highway's off-ramp before my car completely stopped. I was in a very rural area in a time before

*When we're
running on
fumes and don't
stop to refuel,
we'll inevitably
run out of gas.*

cell phones. I felt I had no choice but to abandon my car and start walking. At least there was one light in the distance I could walk toward.

As I got closer, I realized the light was coming from the front porch of a small house. I decided that knocking on the door was my only option. A little old lady answered the door. After I explained my situation from my side of the screen door, she let me in to use her telephone to call my parents. While I waited to be res-

cued, she made me tea and served me sugar cookies. Looking back, I realize this story could have had a tragic ending had there been someone dangerous on the other side of that door. It was dark. I was all alone. No one knew where I was. I was completely vulnerable. I can't tell you how many times I've thanked God that when I was in need, I found someone safe and nurturing to turn to for help.

Running on Fumes
When Martha's tank is on empty from her many tasks of serving, I'm sure there are a lot of people she could have turned to. She could have directly confronted her sister, Mary. She could have complained to her brother, Lazarus. She could have gone next

door and commiserated with her neighbor. Things inside Martha feel dark. She's all alone with her tasks, and her empty tank has her tension running high. She's vulnerable and raw. Had she turned to either of her siblings or her neighbor, the story might have ended differently, probably tragically, for her heart and soul. Fortunately, she's blessed beyond measure that when she needs help, she finds her way from the kitchen back to Jesus in her living room. You can't ask for anyone safer and more nurturing than he. Not only does Jesus welcome her in; he stops everything to focus completely on her and her distress.

However, Jesus doesn't make Martha tea or sugarcoat his response. He wants to give Martha the tools she needs to remain filled at all times: That's how deeply he loves her. It pains him to see her running on fumes. He wants to provide her with the living fuel to do what she needs to do, and go wherever and whenever necessary.

Running on fumes is how we Marthas live. We go and go, like that little Energizer Bunny, thinking our batteries will never run out. We don't value rest. In fact, we see it as a waste of time, something that keeps us from our long list of things to do. Even when we pause for prayer or to reconnect with others, we have one eye on the clock, very mindful of our time spent away from being productive, and we're anxious to get back to doing. Moreover, after putting ourselves last on the list of people to care for, we don't follow through when it's our turn on the list. It feels too self-indulgent. Plus, we're too darn tired by that point to invest any energy in ourselves. It's easier to take a pass on what feels like just another burden and forge ahead instead.

As we forge ahead, we overlook the fact that self-care is a requirement of the golden rule. Matthew 22:37–39 says we should love the Lord our God and our neighbor as ourselves. If we are meant to love our neighbor as ourselves, we must put love of self into action. I believe Sabbath is the space God created for that, making the Sabbath and self-care synonymous. When we misinterpret one, we misinterpret the other, to our own detriment. We Marthas are rule followers. We focus more on the rules of the Sabbath to earn the blessings, rather than on emptying our hands to receive the gifts. Consequently, the Sabbath becomes just another day with a new list of to-dos. Although they're different from our tasks on Monday through Saturday, they're "have-tos" nonetheless: Go to Church, spend time with family, cook a big meal to gather everyone together, visit the people we need to see, prep for the week ahead so there's less work to be tackled then, and so on. As we look around at other people being carefree and doing fun things, we might even grow resentful, viewing the Sabbath as just another empty promise of being renewed.

Valuing Self-Care

As the Master of Creation, God could easily have forged ahead and made the world in a day. But perhaps he knew we Marthas would use that as our excuse to continue striving and doing seven days a week. Ultimately, we'd drive ourselves into the ground. Genesis 2:3 says, "So God blessed the seventh day and hallowed it, because on it God rested from all the work that he had done in creation." Like speed limits and road signs that get us safely where we need to go, our ever-loving Guide slowed himself down to illustrate what the week should look like. Each day, for six days, he was focused and intentional with his work. At the end of every one of those days, he paused, looked back over what he had done, and called it "good" (Gn 1:10). Wanting to fill us to the brim, he also instituted the Sabbath, and then he called it "holy" (Ex 20:8).

The Sabbath concept doesn't have to be restricted to just one day, though. Jesus himself shows us what a Sabbath moment looks like. When he took on our humanity, his energy supply came with a limit. When he was at risk of stalling out, he slept in the back of a boat to recharge (see Mk 4:38) or withdrew to a deserted place to pray (Lk 5:16). No matter what those Sabbath moments looked like, the objective was the same: to rejuvenate and recenter himself in the Father.

I believe that when Jesus tells Martha, "There is need of only one thing," he's talking directly from experience. Having received the gifts that reconnecting with his Father can bring, he wants to promote that concept. Being in his Father's presence is what rejuvenated Jesus, recentered him, and filled him to the brim.

Jesus isn't saying he wants Martha at his feet in adoration to feed his ego. He's saying that God is the source of all. Being one with the Father, Jesus wants to help Martha understand that God is just waiting to give her everything she needs, like a full-service gas station. He doesn't want to help Martha cruise through just the dinner party. He wants to help her cruise through life itself. All she has to do is pull up alongside the pump and connect herself to him. God will do the rest, free of charge, filling her to the brim with a grace that will fuel her through whatever task or journey lies ahead. Jesus knows that when we go to God for true rest, not only are we refilled, but the grace we're filled with radiates out from us, making us radiant in the process. Once Martha allows God to pour his grace into her, she'll possess her own glow. Then there won't be anything she can't do.

That same glow is ours to have if we just honor the Sabbath. Of course, the definition of rest, and even the route to God, will be different for each of us. What is important is that our activities should be different from the tasks we perform all week long. Sabbath is meant to be our day-long coffee break from our work, a chance to look back on what we've accomplished and call it "good." It's also a time to choose activities that rejuvenate. As Mark Buchanan says in his book *The Rest of God: Restoring Your Soul by Restoring Sabbath:* "Sabbath is not for more creating. It is for re-creating."* To help us differentiate between the two, he suggests that, prior to doing an activity, we consider this question: "Is it something you create, or something that re-creates you? Choose the re-creative thing on Sabbath."

We need to give God the chance to bless us, refill us, and renew us. Buchanan goes on to sum up the golden rule of the Sabbath: "Cease from what is necessary. Embrace that which gives life." Naturally, we need to honor the Lord's day by spending time with him in church. As Catholics, this means going to Mass. From there, however, each person's Sabbath activities will differ as much as we differ from one another. What brings one person renewal may seem like work to another, and vice versa. What is critical, however, is choosing our activities with discernment. We need to be sure we're not traveling toward the wrong light. Not everything that looks like rest is intended for our good.

> *Not everything that looks like rest is intended for our good.*

Escape is a perfect example. We should never confuse it with rest. When we escape, we choose activities that are devoid of purpose. After one of these activities, we're no better off when we return to business as usual. Often, we feel worse — lethargic, cranky, with tension humming right below the surface, ready to spike at the slightest provocation.

To avoid this, we have to be mindful of using our activities of choice to reconnect with God. That's how self-care and Sabbath become reprieves from the chaos. They offer a chance to regroup, rejuvenate, and discern what will lead us closer to God.

---

*Mark Buchanan, *The Rest of God: Restoring Your Soul by Restoring Sabbath* (Nashville: Thomas Nelson, 2006), 129.

Observing the Sabbath is about recalibrating things so we remember where and who our true north is. That's how we know in which direction to head when Monday rolls around.

We're blessed by self-care and Sabbath when we choose activities that restore. They provide rest to our bodies, stimulation to our minds, inspiration to our souls, and joy to our hearts. We're the only ones who can determine when we're escaping and when we're restoring. However, there are some criteria and questions to help us define the line between the two:

- **Conscious choice**: Am I consciously deciding to _____ because I think it will bring me joy? Or am I defaulting to it because I have nothing else to do?
- **The process**: While doing _____, are the emotions I feel positive? Or are they negative?
- **Reconnecting with God**: While doing _____, am I mindful of God's being with me in my enjoyment? Or do I forget to include him?
- **End result**: After I've _____, do I feel restored? Or do I feel no better off, perhaps even more depleted?

Over time, it becomes crystal clear that taking time to relax has us returning to our tasks more energized, focused, and productive. That's the paradox of rest: We become doubly productive in half the time when we honor Sabbath and self-care.

Tune-Ups and Tuning In

I'm a slow learner. About five years after I ran out of gas, I was at the tail end of a three-hour drive to see friends when another warning light went off on my dashboard. Actually, two lights: one for the oil and one for the engine. I was between exits and didn't feel like pulling over on the highway. Besides, I was getting close to my destination. I figured I'd have things checked out when I got there. Lo and behold, the engine in my car completely seized. To my horror, the tow truck guy explained that once that happens, it's over! He towed my car to the junk yard, where it became just another heap of scrap metal. Needless to say, I've become quite attentive to warning lights since.

And oh my, there are a lot of warning lights now. Not only are new cars equipped with a bazillion sensors, but they can be synced with email addresses. Once a month, a diagnostic summary of a vehicle's entire operating system can be sent directly to the owner's inbox. Coded in green, yellow, and red, these summaries tell us if all is well, what action is suggested, and what action is immediately required. All the guesswork is gone. We can now prevent minor and serious damage before it even begins.

Sabbath and self-care are two sensors God wants us to sync with our lives. When we practice both, not only do we become restored and rejuvenated, we become more in tune with the different signals in our hearts. We learn how to identify the warning signs in advance so we'll know when we're running out of gas and when something more severe might be wrong. That's how we avoid the serious damage we can cause when we blow a gasket in anger or crash and burn after ignoring the warning signs.

More intricate than any car's engine, each one of us has various needs and multiple personality traits. That doesn't make us schizophrenic. It keeps us balanced, rounding us out. By laying down our tasks for a bit while we intentionally rest, we're able to exhale our tension and breath in God. Indulging in self-care during Sabbath moments gives our Martha side a break and nurtures the Mary within.

At His Feet

Great Rescuer,

Help me to recognize and heed the warning signs that tell me I'm running on fumes. Remind me that you are standing by, at the ready, to fill me to the brim and equip me with what I need. When I'm too stubborn or lazy to respond to the warning signs, remind me that you are the safe and nurturing one I should turn to when I'm in distress. Prompt me to look back and see all the times you've rescued me in the past, as proof of your unfailing love.

Inspire me to follow your lead, laying down my work for a while so I can rest, rejuvenate, and recenter myself in you. Help me to understand that the Sabbath is your gift to me — one that I cannot receive unless I empty my hands to receive it. After I've spent time with you, honoring your day, inspire me to choose life-giving activities that restore me. Prompt me to invite you along for the ride, recognizing that when you witness my joy from the passenger seat, it fills your heart to the brim.

I ask this in Jesus' name. Amen.

Unwrapping the G-I-F-T

Gauge — What are the warning signs when I'm running on fumes? What happens when I ignore them? How does that make me feel?

Invite — What happens when I invite those feelings in and sit with them at God's feet?

Filter — What do I see when I look at the situation through the filter of God's loving eyes?

Transform — Do I value self-care and Sabbath? When can I fit Sabbath moments and self-care into my week? What life-giving activities can I do during that time to restore and rejuvenate myself?

10
Employing Self-Discipline

Mary has chosen the better part, which
will not be taken away from her.
— Luke 10:42

My cousins were some of my best friends growing up. I was doubly blessed because they also happened to be my neighbors. Christine lived in the house diagonally across from mine; Lorna lived down the street. Lorna was one of the first kids in the neighborhood to get a swimming pool — one of those big, oval, above-ground pools we couldn't wait to jump into. Our favorite thing to do was create a whirlpool in it. We'd get a big group of kids, space ourselves out in the water, and begin running around the edge of the pool, all going in the same direction. The beginning was always the hardest. Static things tend to resist change. When faced with resistance, you have to double your efforts in order to move forward.

The more laps we did, the more we created a current that moved along with us, making it easier and easier to go in that direction. Once we built the current as strong as we could, someone would yell, "Reverse!" We'd all turn around and head in the opposite direction, or at least we'd try. On the days we felt powerful, we'd dig deep for the strength and muscle we needed to reverse things, cheering each other on to success. Other days, we'd take the lazy (and far more fun) route of kicking up our heels, lying on our backs, and letting the current we had created carry us along.

Resisting Self-Control

I suspect that Martha and Mary start out creating a current together when they hear that Jesus is coming to dinner. They're sisters, after all. I like to imagine them cooperating in the beginning, going in the same direction, picking up momentum as they move around the house, getting ready for the dinner party. If they are moving in the same direction together, Mary must realize shortly after Jesus arrives that she doesn't want to continue in that current anymore. Although she's expected to serve, it's as if she hears the "reverse" command in her head when she feels herself being pulled away from Jesus, not toward him. For his part, Jesus knows the resistance Mary is up against with the cultural norms.

Yet Mary's desire to be at Jesus' feet runs so deep, she's willing to defy the pressure to conform. She knows she needs a new current, one that will pull her toward him, not away. So she figures out a plan and then executes it. Using self-discipline, she digs her heels in, stops moving in the direction that's wrong for her, does an about-face, and moves, step by step, against the push of the old flow. The old current is strong, but her resolve is stronger. It keeps her going in the new direction, one that's right for her now. With every step she takes, the new momentum builds. She doesn't stop until she gets to the feet of Jesus. It's important to note that it's not the plan that's the key to Mary's success; it's her use of self-discipline in executing it. We're never what we plan. We are what we do. Good or bad, our actions define us. We should want them to refine us.

Once Mary is at the feet of Jesus, her heart swells with peace and rightness when Jesus speaks. It's that peace and rightness that doubles her resolve to stay the course. Even if she were to feel any pull from Martha in the kitchen, the reward of Mary's efforts "will not be taken away from her." Not only has she used self-discipline to draw closer to God, but she uses self-discipline to stay there. Awash in joy and firmly established in the new momentum that's right for her now, she kicks back for a bit and lets Jesus' words buoy her along.

> *We're never what we plan. We are what we do.*

Perhaps Martha feels the same tug of the "reverse" command that Mary did. Unfortunately, it seems that Martha resists it. She has a list of things she wants to do, and she builds a momentum going in the wrong direction with each task she undertakes. The resulting whirlpool pulls her further and further away from where she's supposed to be. Moreover, her heart goes adrift when she forgets her intention of doing it all for Jesus. It's then that she allows resentment for her sister to take over, dragging her toward a vortex of tension — one that seems to have a life force all its own.

When we Marthas start moving, we're a force to be reckoned with. The more we push forward with our plans, the more of a current we create. As the momentum carries us along, we get so excited by our progress that we don't stop to question whether the progress we're making is meaningful or meant for us. If and when we do realize we're getting carried further away from who we want to be, the idea of reversing direction is overwhelming. We know how much energy and strength it's going to take to stop, do an about-face, push back against the habits we've created, and move in the right direction. Despite the momentum going in the direction that's wrong for us, it seems so much easier to give in and let the bad current take us away.

When we feel the pull of a bad current, God yearns for us to resist. He made us free, and he longs for us to enjoy that freedom. When Egypt enslaved the Israelites, God sent Moses to lead them out. When the chains of original sin ensnared humanity, God sent Jesus to break them, once and for all, on the cross. Now it's up to us to protect our own freedom. The challenge is that slavery comes in so many forms, we don't always recognize it as such.

I propose that, in today's world, what threatens our freedom most is our own emotions, and our self-indulgence in them, something Galatians 5:13 warns against: "You were called to freedom, brothers and sisters; only do not use your freedom as an opportunity for self-indulgence." Yet society has put so much emphasis on emotions, we've raised them up and made them gods. The constant message we're bombarded with is: *If something feels good, do it.* Conversely, if something causes us discomfort, we're encouraged to walk away. There's no focus on consequences, giving us permission to ignore doing the right thing. The more we subscribe to this philosophy, the more we make emotions the master of our lives. We let anger raise our voices and fists. We give lethargy permission to keep us stuck in one place. We empower pleasure to erase our moral compass. We allow self-pity to feed our vices. By giving our emotions permission to pull us along in their current, we risk falling into the Bermuda Triangle of time: We wake up one morning and find that our good intentions and dreams have inexplicably disappeared. All we're left with is a shipwreck of bad choices in a sea of negative emotions.

Sadly, this cycle of letting our emotions rule us picks up momentum as it goes. The problem with any momentum is that it's hard to stop, no matter what direction it's going in. That's when we need to circle back, as Martha did, to Jesus. If Jesus could calm the storm with just a word (Mk 4:39), he can stop the momentum of whatever bad cycle we're in. He can also help us understand the double standard of emotions: Where tension and negative emotions seem to rise out of nowhere, tempting us down the wrong path, positive emotions come only as a result of positive actions. Moving in the right direction is a decision. It's only *after* we take a step in the right direction that we begin to feel the positive effects that propel us forward. If we wait around for the desire, energy, or inspiration to stop our bad behavior, we'll never break the cycle of going with the wrong flow.

The problem with any momentum is that it's hard to stop, no matter what direction it's going in.

Employing Self-Discipline

The perfect example of what it looks like to resist the wrong flow is Jesus. He never drifted with any current that went against his Father's plan. In fact, he was always doing the opposite of what people expected. He was the Son of God, yet he came to serve. He was the Messiah, yet he ate with tax collectors and prostitutes. He was born a king, yet he knelt and washed the feet of his apostles. He did whatever it took to bring people to his Father, no matter how strong the tide went in the opposite direction. Possessing our human nature, he knew to employ self-discipline when confronting anything that tried to pull him the wrong way. That alone should teach us that we, too, need to use the tool of self-discipline when reversing any bad current we're in.

Keeping with the theme of whirlpools, I looked up the physics behind them. Honestly, it went right over my head. To simplify things, we'll talk about breaking the cycle of any bad momentum by using basic math terms: *product, equals sign, equation, add, subtract, divide, and multiply.* Before we figure out what we need to do, we have to figure out what we want the end *product* to be. What do we want on the other side of the *equals sign*? What result are we looking for? Once we know, we can begin writing the steps of the *equation* to get there. Most of us already know what to do, but spending time at Jesus' feet in prayer always gives more clarity about the specifics.

Typically, in order to be successful, we need to *add* in whatever we're lacking. We aren't meant to go it alone. The more supportive people and things we can bring into our lives, the higher our success rate will be. Conversely, there are times when we need to *subtract* whatever is pulling us the wrong way. If we want to change direction, yet everyone else in the pool is still going the way that's wrong for us, we may need to switch pools. Even Jesus commanded us to shake the dust from our feet when people or things become toxic (see Mt 10:14).

In the same vein, we need to *divide* our expectations: Before making any plan for change, we need to be sensible about our current situation. If we plan to go to the gym every day in pursuit of a healthier lifestyle, yet we have a nursing baby at home, we're not going to meet our goal. If we declare we're never taking another work call while spending time with family, yet we're the key player on a big deal about to close, we're going to let someone down when the phone rings. We can't set ourselves up for failure by expecting too much, especially in the beginning. It's impossible to reverse any momentum all at once. If we try, we'll waste all our strength and energy right at the start, burning it up in a blaze of glory, only to be left exhausted and vulnerable to a negative cycle again. It's fine to go big-picture with our hopes and dreams, keeping our eyes on the prize of the end goal, but we need to go small-picture with our actions. It's only by putting one foot in front of the other, one step at a time, that we'll ever get anywhere.

Lastly, we need to *multiply* it all by God. Everything expands when he's involved. Not only does he surround us with an overall pool of support, but he gets as specific with his help as we need him to be. None of us is complete. We all have our shortcomings. If we turn to God for what we lack, he'll give us everything we need to get where we need to go.

The Strongest Current

When God created the oceans, he gave them strong currents to move everything where it needs to be. Like conveyor belts, currents carry the equator's heat to the North and South Poles, bring food and nutrients to the marine ecosystem, and push ocean life to new places. Discipleship works this way too. It's as if God wove the concept into nature itself to inspire us to follow Jesus. When we do, we carry the warmth of his love to the world. We feed hungry bodies and souls through our service and prayers. And we ourselves are pushed into new places so we will grow in all the best ways.

As if the currents weren't enough to make his point, we have the *way* and the *how* woven into our very language. *Disciple* and *discipline* have the same Latin root, *discipulus*, meaning "pupil." A student learns from her teacher. As Lindsay Schlegel writes in her book *Don't Forget to Say Thank You: And Other Parenting Lessons that Brought Me Closer to God*, "Being a disciple is about being trained by someone who knows the way."* Jesus knew that the *way* was to do his Father's will, not his own (see Jn 6:38). He also knew that the *how* was through self-discipline. God's will for

---

*Lindsay Schlegel, *Don't Forget to Say Thank You: And Other Parenting Lessons that Brought Me Closer to God* (Notre Dame, IN: Ave Maria Press, 2018), 19.

us is to prosper. How we achieve that is by laying down our resistance to self-control and diving into the pool of God's grace for the self-discipline we need.

Self-Discipline: The Remedy for Mid-Level Tension

It's important that we began the discussion of mid-level tension with the chapter on boundaries. Once we draw healthy boundaries, the other areas of mid-level tension become easier to identify and easier to tackle. It's equally important to end the discussion of mid-level tension with this chapter on self-discipline. We can talk all we want about making plans to respond to God's prompts for change. But if we don't use self-discipline in carrying them out, they're all just words on the page. That's why boundaries and self-discipline make good bookends for addressing mid-level tension: They prop up all the other strategies and hold them all together.

Of the two, however, self-discipline is by far the more important one. In fact, it's the key to success in resolving any mid-level tension. Using self-discipline prevents us from remaining mired in our stress by propelling us forward with our plans for change. Without it, we'd face serious ramifications in our lives, just as the planet would if the ocean currents stopped. Applying self-discipline in all the ways we want to change ensures that we don't run hot when we should run cold, the good in us is fed so we can continue to thrive, and the current we're moving in pulls us closer to God.

∙∙

At His Feet

Wonderful Teacher,

Help me understand that it's your will for me to prosper. Reveal to me all the ways I prevent your grace from leading me there. Give me the strength I need to stop myself from going in the direction that's wrong for me and make an about-face. Don't let me be discouraged by the resistance I face as I move, step by step, against the tide. Protect me from the pull of my bad habits and anyone who tries to draw me down the wrong path. Surround me with your love and a good support network so I may make steady and lasting progress.

Once I've aligned my choices and actions with your will and I'm firmly established in the momentum that's right for me, remind me, every once in a while, to kick up my heels with gratitude, lie on my back, and let all you've blessed me with buoy me along.

I ask this in Jesus' name. Amen.

_____

Unwrapping the G-I-F-T

Gauge — What currents are pulling me in the wrong direction? How do I feel when I resist self-control, giving in to what's easy?

Invite — What happens when I invite those feelings in and sit with them at God's feet?

Filter — What do I see when I look at the situation through the filter of God's loving eyes?

Transform — How do I go about applying the "math words" of self-discipline to reverse the currents that aren't right for me?

11
Reclaiming Our Choice

Now a certain man was ill, Lazarus of Bethany, the
village of Mary and her sister Martha. Mary was the one
who anointed the Lord with perfume and wiped his feet
with her hair; her brother Lazarus was ill. So the sisters
sent a message to Jesus, "Lord, he whom you love is ill."
— John 11:1–3

When my sons, Zack and Mason, were five and three (and my daughter, Jocelyn, was just a wish in my heart), they began playing with Planet Heroes action figures. The hand-me-down toys were from an older cousin and were long since discontinued. When my boys' obsession had them adding to their Christmas list every Planet Heroes hero and villain they didn't yet have, I had to scour Craigslist and buy the toys secondhand.

The next challenge came when it was time to wrap them. Obviously, I didn't have the original boxes. So I put them in old instant-oatmeal boxes, shoe boxes, any kind of box I could get my hands on. Then I wrapped them in fun Christmas paper and hid them away until the big day.

I will never forget Zack and Mason's reactions as they unwrapped those old, recycled boxes on Christmas morning. Even at the age of three, Mason could arch one eyebrow at a time. He did just that as he wailed, "What! Santa got me oatmeal for Christmas?" Then he pushed the unopened box away in disgust. He reached for the next wrapped gift with the hope of redemption. Zack did the same (minus the eyebrow arch — it's not in his genetic makeup). They unwrapped two gifts each before Zack finally caught on and looked inside one of the boxes. There were shrieks of joy and elation from that point on as they realized they *did* get what they wanted for Christmas.

Feeling We Have No Choice

Thus far, we've learned that low-level tension dissolves when we respond to God's gentle nudge. We've also learned that when we don't respond, or when we choose a response that's wrong (or a right response with a wrong intention), our tension spikes to mid-level. When that happens, it's by taking our stress to God that we discover what the right response would have been. Once we make that new *outward* change and align our hearts with it, our tension dissolves.

Now we'll move on to high-level tension. This type of strain results from the extreme situation in which our choice seems to be taken away: the cancer diagnosis, the layoff from work, the loss of a loved one, and so forth. We view these situations as my kids did those old oatmeal boxes on Christmas morning. We take one look, raise an eyebrow, wail that God has abandoned us, and push them away with disgust. Isaiah

11:3 cautions: "He shall not judge by what his eyes see, / or decide by what his ears hear." When we judge things by their outward appearance, we miss out on what's inside. God is the original Santa Claus. He doesn't hand out coal or recycled anything. He loves effusively and unconditionally. He's constantly showering us with new and amazing gifts. It breaks his heart when we leave them unopened.

Reclaiming Our Choice

At the dinner party in Luke 10, Jesus had gifts and lessons for both sisters. He layered those gifts and lessons within his words and within the tension that drew them both to him in the first place. Each sister had the choice to receive them, open them, and apply them. I believe both did, and both were transformed in the process.

When we judge things by their outward appearance, we miss out on what's inside.

Now we'll see those transformations play out as we move on to where the sisters appear next in Scripture: John 11 and John 12. In these passages, Martha and Mary will show us that we do, in fact, have a choice in high-level tension. Although we may not be able to make *outward* changes in certain circumstances, we'll learn from the sisters how to reclaim our choice and use it to make *inward* changes, dissolving our high-level tension in the process. It's a more challenging undertaking, for sure, but the first step is always reaching out to Jesus for help. The sisters model this for us in the midst of their own severe tension. When their brother Lazarus is ill, they send for Jesus, seeking his help in the midst of their pain. In his perfect timing, he responds, leading them through their anguish after Lazarus dies. Witnessing the results of this will inspire us to follow Martha and Mary's lead in reaching out to Jesus in our own pain and heartbreak. If we do so, he'll help us work through our extreme tension so we, too, will be able to enjoy the peace and joy God tucks inside everything.

The Perfect Match

For the lesser holidays, such as Valentine's Day and Saint Patrick's Day, I like to buy one small gift for each of my kids. I usually get them all the same thing so it's clear I'm not favoring one over another. To add to the giving and to stretch out the joy, I individualize things by creating a different treasure hunt for each child. They have to solve them in order to find their gifts. Clue after clue has them going from room to room, upstairs and down, and occasionally outside.

My kids love the presents at the end, of course. But they're equally thrilled by the hunt. Knowing I've invested love and effort to create clues very specific to each one of them makes them feel affirmed in their unique interests and appreciated for how differently they think. As any parent will tell you, even though multiple kids are raised in the same home, with the same parents, and with the same rules, our kids are like snowflakes: Each is a one-of-a-kind creation. When we take the time to value and honor each child as an individual, the process itself becomes another gift. I don't always hit the nail on the head with every treasure hunt I create. But when I do, there's no greater satisfaction than making that perfect match.

God knows each one of us intimately, more than we know ourselves. He's fully aware of our individual circumstances, and he understands exactly how we think. When high-level tension strikes, he's never the source of it. But he does know what gift to tuck inside it to match our specific need. Furthermore, the path he marks out for each one of us to walk when applying that gift is unique to each of us. He created us. He knows our individual style as well as the pace at which we process. He values and honors it all, right down to the last detail of our unique situation. Nothing is a challenge for God. No matter how complicated we can be, he hits the nail on the head every time. Yet it still brings him immense satisfaction when we apply his gifts and he sees just how perfectly he matches us with peace and joy.

At His Feet

Wondrous Giver of Gifts,

When I'm faced with an overwhelming hardship, help me realize that you are never to blame. You send only good things my way, out of an abundance of compassion and mercy. Remind me, in the midst of my challenge, that you also provide exactly what I need to get me through. Remove my judgment so I will recognize the gift you've placed within my struggle. Be with me as I open it and look inside. Fill me with whatever I need to apply that gift to my situation, using it like a salve for my broken heart and weary soul.

After you've led me through my difficult time, remind me to look back and recognize that, in my darkest hour, you knew precisely how to comfort me. Help me identify all the ways you shaped my journey to suit exactly who I am, lifting me up at my lowest point by making me feel affirmed and valued. Inspire me to return to you in gratitude, ever mindful that you are the source of love itself, a love that won't rest until my heart is healed.

I ask this in Jesus' name. Amen.

Unwrapping the G-I-F-T

Gauge — Am I facing any hardship that has me overwhelmed? Is it stirring up any other emotions?

Invite — What happens when I invite those feelings in and sit with them at God's feet?

Filter — What do I see when I look at the situation through the filter of God's loving eyes?

Transform — Do I believe that God is never the source of the hardships I face? What is the gift God is giving me in the midst of it? How do I go about applying that gift to my life?

12
Adjusting Expectations

But when Jesus heard it, he said, "This illness does not lead to death; rather it is for God's glory, so that the Son of God may be glorified through it." Accordingly, though Jesus loved Martha and her sister and Lazarus, after having heard that Lazarus was ill, he stayed two days longer in the place where he was. ...

When Jesus arrived, he found that Lazarus had already been in the tomb four days. Now Bethany was near Jerusalem, some two miles away, and many of the Jews had come to Martha and Mary to console them about their brother. When Martha heard that Jesus was coming, she went and met him, while Mary stayed home. Martha said to Jesus, "Lord, if you had been here, my brother would not have died. But even now I know that

> *God will give you whatever you ask of him." Jesus said to*
> *her, "Your brother will rise again." Martha said to him,*
> *"I know that he will rise again in the resurrection on the*
> *last day." Jesus said to her, "I am the resurrection and*
> *the life. Those who believe in me, even though they die,*
> *will live, and everyone who lives and believes in me will*
> *never die. Do you believe this?" She said to him, "Yes,*
> *Lord, I believe that you are the Messiah, the Son of God,*
> *the one coming into the world."*
> *— John 11:4–6, 17–27*

The open-air markets in Guatemala are stunning, especially in the indigenous villages. Filled with the most vivid and intricately woven tapestries in the world, they're a tourist's dream. Unlike a retail store, however, there are no price tags. Instead, they use the oldest form of pricing known to man: haggling. Haggling is when the buyer throws out a price far lower than she knows she'll get. The seller does the same on the high end. This is followed by the negotiation dance, in which each party takes slow, compromising steps to meet in the middle. The haggling I witnessed was always amicable and in good fun.

The exception was when an entitled foreigner stepped into the picture. Unfortunately, there was always that person who demanded that the world work according to him. Inevitably, he'd demand a price too low and wouldn't budge, insulting the vendor in the process. Seeing the disaster before it happened, the vendor would pull back his goods and turn his back, signaling that the exchange was over. The entitled one was always too clueless to read the signs or see how irrational he was being. Instead, he'd start ranting about how unfair the vendor was being.

The rest of us foreigners would shudder with embarrassment. It was clear to us how irrational the entitled one was being. He was asking too much. If, for some reason, the vendor did acquiesce, we knew he was doing so at a loss to himself and to the artist who wove the piece. It broke my heart whenever a vendor gave in to an unreasonable demand. Not only was he undercutting himself; he was also enabling the selfish behavior of the entitled one. I wished there were some gentle process that would magically teach that tourist a better way.

Demanding Miracles

Jesus teaches us a better way so we're not guilty of demanding things from God like the entitled tourist. In John 11, Martha and Mary send word to Jesus that their brother, Lazarus, is ill. They don't flat-out ask Jesus to perform a miracle, and by no means do they demand it, but they sure do infer it. They add to the exchange by reminding Jesus of his love for their brother. They don't mean to manipulate him, nor do they see this as a negotiation tactic. Their love for Jesus runs too deep for that. They know that real love is never transactional. But the sisters' overwhelming concern for their brother has them desperate and assuming. They've known Jesus

Real love is never transactional.

for years. They're well aware of the countless miracles he's performed. They presume that once Jesus knows that Lazarus is ill, it's fair to expect that Jesus will heal him. It never occurs to them that what they're asking for may be unreasonable.

For his part, Jesus would love to acquiesce and heal Lazarus immediately. However, he's privy to the bigger picture. He knows that performing the miracle right away won't lead to his Father's glory later (see Jn 11:4). He'd never undercut God. That's too high a price to pay. So, despite his deep love for Lazarus and the sisters, the exchange ends there.

It's tempting to approach prayer like a negotiation, especially when it comes to something extreme, such as the life of a loved one. In our desire to get what we want, we may unconsciously weave manipulation into our prayer, as if we can haggle with God: *If you cure my brother's cancer, I'll go to church every week and volunteer at the soup kitchen.* We presume there's some sort of negotiation dance in which God and we take slow, compromising steps to meet in the middle. We may also throw in the "love" card to stack the deck: *If you're truly a loving God, you'll heal my child.* The more extreme the situation, the more desperate we become. The more desperate we become, the more prone we are to demanding a miracle.

God welcomes our bold prayers and places no limits on what we can ask. Once we do ask, however, we're to place it in his hands, letting go of the outcome, trusting he'll answer in the way that's best for us, according to his will. When we place restrictions on how he can respond, requiring him to do things exactly our way, we cross the line of asking and move into the realm of demanding. Judith 8:16 clearly spells out: "Do not try to bind the purpose of the Lord our God; for God is not like a human being, to be threatened, or like a mere mortal, to be won over by pleading."

When we do make demands, we overlook the fact that we don't know the bigger picture, nor are we always meant to. Of course, God is a loving God and wants nothing more than for all of us to be well and filled with peace. However, we don't always see what will lead to that end. God is the only one with the holy perspective to know. Whereas we view things in the short-term, God views them in the long-term. Whereas we fixate on the temporal, he focuses on the eternal. He'll never sell us short with a miracle now that would deny us our full glory later. He loves us too much for that and won't negotiate.

Jesus doesn't negotiate with Martha and Mary either. Only after Lazarus has been in the tomb for four days does Jesus finally arrive in Bethany. Martha, in her usual "go get 'em" style, doesn't wait for Jesus to arrive at the house. She goes out to meet him. The first words she greets him with are "Lord, if you had been here, my brother would not have died" (Jn 11:21). Not the warmest of welcomes, that's for sure. But Martha always speaks her mind to Jesus, as we all should. Real relationship means being real with our thoughts and our emotions. It's what leads Martha to be her bold self and resume the negotiation dance. She tells Jesus, "But even now I know that God will give you whatever you ask of him" (Jn 11:22). I'm sure Martha wishes she could have done away with the pain of Lazarus's death, but she's willing to compromise and accept Jesus bringing him back to life now.

For his part, Jesus offers her something better: the fact that Lazarus will rise on the last day (see v. 23). Martha realizes she can't ask for more than for her brother to be with God for all eternity. Consequently, she adjusts her expectations. In doing so, she positions herself to receive a "Bonus Miracle." A Bonus Miracle is the additional gift God bestows on us when we accept his will. It's the transformation that occurs in our hearts and minds when we stop begging for what cannot be. Once Martha let's go of her demands, her Bonus Miracle changes her tension into peace knowing her brother will live in glory with God.

But Jesus doesn't stop there. He wants to bless Martha with more and says, "I am the resurrection and the life. Those who believe in me, even though they die, will live, and everyone who lives and believes in me will never die. Do you believe this? *(see Jn 11:25–26).* It's in that moment that she receives an even greater Bonus Miracle: the realization of exactly who Jesus is. The realization is so profound, she'll never be the same again. In a statement of faith that infuses her very soul, she responds with, "Yes, Lord, I believe that you are the Messiah, the Son of God, the one coming into the world" (Jn 11:27). Receiving abundantly more than she could ever haggle for, she ends the exchange there. She has no idea there's more to the story.

In the next chapter, we'll see what unfolds with Lazarus. But suffice it to say, a story is never over until the main character of faith resides in heaven with God. There are countless examples of God's hand at work well after the ending seems to have been written. Although Peter denied Jesus three times and thought all was lost after the crucifixion, he went on to become the head of the Church. When Paul and Silas were flogged, thrown into prison, shackled to the floor, and guarded by jailers, it looked as if they'd never get out. Yet an earthquake shook the ground, opened all the cell doors, and loosened their chains. Best of all, after Jesus died on the cross and lay in a tomb for three days, he rose from the dead and has been with us ever since. God never once ignored these people when they cried out for help in the thick of their pain. In fact, I believe their pain was only a fraction of the anguish he felt looking down on them. But he knew that acquiescing to their pleas too soon would rob them of their greater victories later.

The same holds true for us. In the thick of our pain, I believe God's heart splits in two. When he doesn't acquiesce to our demands, it's not out of a lack of love, but out of an abundance of it. He knows the glory yet to come. He won't undercut that or compromise the ending by writing it too soon.

Adjusting Expectations

All the twists and turns and cliffhangers in our storyline *will* lead to a happy ending, if we just let God write it. But that can't happen if we're still grasping the pen, scribbling demands, lamenting what we can't have. We can't be the entitled tourist in the open-air market. We have to accept that sometimes the price of what we're asking for is too high. Regardless, the exchange doesn't have to end there. God is offering us a Bonus Miracle all the time: the healing of our hearts and minds. It's only by letting our demands and tension go to him that our hearts and minds will be free to receive that healing.

When we adjust our expectations and accept what God is willing to give, the Bonus Miracles abound. Suddenly, new and wondrous things bless our lives in ways we never could have imagined. It's seeing the loved one we lost in the eyes of the newborn who comes after — not a reincarnation, of course, but a similarity so profound, our hearts recognize the essence of the one we lost living on. It's the change in professional status that, at first, seems a demotion, only to turn out to be the best thing that has ever happened to us. It's the medical condition that becomes a wake-up call to stop taking everyone and everything for granted. There's always a gift tucked inside the tension. We just need to remove the blindfolds of demands and complaints to see it. Hand over the pen. Let God do the writing. When given our complete trust, he'll craft an ending to our story far better than we could ever come up with on our own.

To find the steps for adjusting our expectations, we need only look to Martha. She is our role model for letting go of our demands and being grateful for what God has in store for us. First, we have to make room. Like Martha, we need to be real with God. He's never insulted by what we ask or what we demand. He welcomes our being bold with our requests. He wants to hear about every emotion we feel, whether good or bad. But then we have to let go of the outcome, never placing restrictions on how God can respond. It's only by laying it all at his feet and trusting his will for us that we make room to receive anything new.

Next, we have to open our hands. Once our minds and hearts are heard, we need to sit with God, our feet on the floor, our hands open on our laps, palms up. Just as it's difficult to sneeze with our eyes open, it's almost impossible to feel tension when our hands are physically open to God. It's also how we receive the peace and blessings he wants to give us. That occurs most when we're counting our blessings. One by one, we need to take stock of the good things in our lives, thanking God for each one of them. Gratitude strengthens our immunity to tension. It's hard to see what we don't have when our eyes are fixed on what we do.

It's hard to see what we don't have when our eyes are fixed on what we do.

Lastly, we need to reflect back. Once our crisis has passed, it's critical to look back to identify the good that came as a result of the hardship. The more often we do this, the better we get at identifying the Bonus Miracles God blesses us with constantly. Adding these miracles to our gratitude list strengthens our hope so it will endure through the next challenge we face.

What's Meant to Be

eBay is our First World version of an open-air market. When we see what we want on the website, we type in a bid. As with the haggling in Guatemala, we know that the amount we begin with will most likely increase during the back and forth. That's the fun of the game. The difference is, we're not haggling with the seller. We're haggling with other buyers, like a virutal auction. Up and up the price goes as we take turns outbidding one another. If we get too caught up in the heat of it all, things can get out of hand. Sometimes, we're left paying a price we can't afford. So we put it on our credit card and have to make payments long after we get what we wanted.

There is another option on eBay: the "Buy It Now" feature.

With just the click of a button, we can pay a fixed price and skip all the haggling. Yes, we forgo the chance to reduce the price, but we can see up front what's really in our price range. Then, by adjusting our expectations and being flexible in what we purchase, we can typically get our needs met without going into debt.

I was terrible at haggling in Guatemala, for fear of taking advantage. So I always let the seller set a fixed price. Consequently, a lot of things I wanted ended up being out of my price range, forcing me to choose alternate items instead. Yet, when I look back at what I bought and have kept all these years, I can't remember any of those items I wasn't able to get. They're overshadowed by the joy I feel when I look at the tapestries I was able to buy. Those tapestries teach a lesson that goes far beyond the marketplace: They're a visual reminder to let go of what isn't meant for us and to cherish what is.

....

At His Feet

Glorious Author of All,

In the midst of any difficulty and pain, fill me with the surety that you do hear my cries for help. Surround me with your compassion. Infuse me with your light. Help me trust that I can be real with you, pouring out my thoughts and feelings, no matter how bad or demanding. Once I've done so and have emptied my mind and heart of all expectations, keep me in your loving embrace. Remind me to remain open and empty, giving the pen to you so you can keep writing my story.

Once my crisis is over, give me the eyes to see the past healings that came only when I let go of my demands and trusted your will for me. As that new perspective reveals the Bonus Miracles that abound in my life, prompt me to return to you with gratitude for each and every one of them.

I ask this in Jesus' name. Amen.

Unwrapping the G-I-F-T

Gauge — Is there a miracle I've been demanding of God? How do I feel when it seems he isn't meeting that demand?

Invite — What happens when I invite those feelings in and sit with them at God's feet?

Filter — What do I see when I look at the situation through the filter of God's loving eyes?

Transform — How can I let go of my demands and adjust my expectations? How do I go about increasing my trust in God, allowing him to keep writing my story? When I look back over past difficulties, can I see the Bonus Miracles God has blessed me with?

13
Accepting the Unresolvable

When she [Martha] had said this, she went back and
called her sister Mary, and told her privately, "The
Teacher is here and is calling for you." And when she
heard it, she got up quickly and went to him. Now Jesus
had not yet come to the village, but was still at the place
where Martha had met him. The Jews who were with
her in the house, consoling her, saw Mary get up quickly
and go out. They followed her because they thought that
she was going to the tomb to weep there. When Mary
came where Jesus was and saw him, she knelt at his feet
and said to him, "Lord, if you had been here, my brother
would not have died." When Jesus saw her weeping and
the Jews who came with her also weeping, he was greatly
disturbed in spirit and deeply moved. He said, "Where
have you laid him?" They said to him, "Lord, come and

see." Jesus began to weep. So the Jews said, "See how he
loved him!" But some of them said, "Could not he who
opened the eyes of the blind man have kept this man
from dying?" Then Jesus, again greatly disturbed, came
to the tomb. It was a cave, and a stone was lying against
it. Jesus said, "Take away the stone." Martha, the sister
of the dead man, said to him, "Lord, already there is a
stench because he has been dead four days." Jesus said
to her, "Did I not tell you that if you believe, you would
see the glory of God?" So they took away the stone. And
Jesus looked upward and said "Father, I thank you for
having heard me. I knew that you always hear me, but
I have said this for the sake of the crowd standing here,
so that they may believe that you sent me." When he
had said this, he cried with a loud voice, "Lazarus, come
out!" The dead man came out, his hands and feet bound
with strips of cloth, and his face wrapped in a cloth. Jesus
said to them, "Unbind him, and let him go."
— John 11:28–44

When churches finally opened to the public after the COVID-19 shutdown in 2020, we all had to wear masks for the entire Mass. That first time, I made sure we went prepared. I brought the fabric mask I'd gotten earlier from one of our fellow parishioners. My kids brought the masks that my friend Meagan graciously sewed for them. Up to that point, I'd been out in public with my mask on for only five or ten minutes at a time, ducking into a store for a gallon of milk or the post office for a book of stamps. Those quick errands didn't give me time to register the fact that my mask had shrunk in the wash. The elastic now curled my ears, and the two layers of fabric pulled tight across my nose and mouth.

After just twenty minutes of wearing my now-too-small

mask during Mass, I noticed it was becoming harder and harder to breathe. All my attention began to shift from the priest to my struggle. The more I obsessed, the more claustrophobic I got, taking quick, shallow breaths that were making me lightheaded. Although I was using something that was supposed to keep me safe, it felt as if it were suffocating me. I had gone to church to find peace and comfort, yet I found myself breaking out in a cold sweat, teetering on the edge of passing out.

The intensity of my reaction was a prompt, telling me I needed to make a change. Although I didn't want to distract the other parishioners, I felt I had no choice but to get up, go to the gathering space in the back, and get one of the disposable paper masks on a table there. The moment I slipped that larger, thinner mask on, calm washed over me. Although I would have preferred no mask at all, at least this one allowed me to breathe. I was finally able to accept and relax into the "new normal." Shifting my attention back to the priest and God's presence, I soon forgot about the mask altogether and was filled with the peace I went there for.

Fighting in Denial

Neither Martha nor Mary is filled with peace when Jesus finally makes it to Bethany. They've lost their brother Lazarus, and their hearts are broken. The sisters greet Jesus at different times but with the same words: "Lord, if you had been here, my brother would not have died." Their approaches, however, couldn't be more different. Martha rushes out to meet Jesus, while Mary doesn't go to him until Martha tells her that the Teacher is calling for her (see Jn 11:28). Martha confronts Jesus at eye level, while Mary drops to her knees, humbly lifting her eyes to his. Martha uses the statement to convey her frustration at Jesus' inaction, while Mary uses the words to express her denial over the loss of her loved one. Then Mary weeps. We know her despair is intense and all-consuming because Jesus is "greatly disturbed in spirit and deeply moved" by it (v. 33). In fact, we'll see later that it's Jesus' reaction that helps Mary move beyond denial so she doesn't stay stuck in it. We all know grief is necessary when we lose someone or something we care deeply about. But when we pull it too tight around us, trapping ourselves in the stage of denial, it leaves no room for the breath of new life. It takes what's meant to heal and uses it to suffocate.

When we let the threads of fear wrap around our heart, they always shrink, curling us deeper into fear's web, pulling it tight across our mind.

Neither masks nor tension were ever intended to suffocate us. In fact, both are meant to keep us safe. Take tension in the form of fear, for example. It's actually a warning signal that something's not right. When we figure out the problem and address it (using the G-I-F-T approach), fear is no longer necessary, and it's dissolved by the process.

If we skip a step, however, or avoid the process altogether, fear can steal our breath, choking out new life. Moreover, the mere act of not resolving fear actually feeds it. As it grows, it weaves its way into everything. When we let the threads of fear wrap around our heart, they always shrink, curling us deeper into fear's web, pulling it tight across our mind. Before we know it, we allow it to taint everything. Our world inevitably reduces to just that one, all-consuming emotion, with joy nowhere to be found.

In the book of Exodus, the Israelites' world had been reduced to slavery in Egypt. God sent ten plagues to convince Pharaoh to let them go. We could ask: "If God is all powerful, couldn't he have succeeded with just one plague?" I've heard it said that whenever God chooses a longer process, it's to further illustrate just how impossible a situation is. When the problem is finally resolved, we know with complete certainly that it was by his power. If Pharaoh had relented after just a plague or two, history would have altered the story, making Pharaoh the hero for having compassion on the Israelites. Instead, with each plague, Pharaoh's heart hardened even more (see Ex 7:22), making the release of the Israelites even more unlikely, except by God's mighty hand.

The same is true in the story of Lazarus. Jesus could have cured him, even from a distance, the minute he got word Lazarus was ill. Instead, Jesus lets Lazarus die and then waits two more days to begin the two-day journey to Bethany (see Jn 11:6). Finally there, Jesus asks for the stone to be rolled back from the tomb where Lazarus is buried. Martha intervenes, reminding him that the stench will be horrific, as Lazarus has been dead for four days (v. 39).

We might at first view this story as long and drawn out, but Jesus sees each aspect as part of the process. Martha presumes that the death, the wait, and the stench all point to finality. Jesus knows that every detail will point to God's sovereignty. Nothing is impossible for the one who reigns over everything. Sure enough, when the stone is rolled back, and Jesus commands, "Lazarus, come out" (v. 43), Lazarus rises and comes out of the tomb.

Accepting the Unresolvable

We will all face our three or four days in the tomb. Life has its hardships that cannot be escaped. Regardless of how dark our cave, or the duration of our time in it, we need to trust that God is working to bring us back to life. Resurrecting us is a process, and it cannot be rushed. It's the process, in fact, that molds and reshapes us for the new way of life God has planned for us. We have to feel the pain, accept the unresolvable, work our way through the steps, and be transformed by it all. It's only then that God will roll back the stone, call us forward, and lead us into a new light — one that glows with renewed hope for what can be.

Both Martha and Mary experience this transformation. First, they must spend time going through the five stages of grief, though, working their way through denial, anger, bargaining, depression, and finally acceptance. As we saw in chapter 12, Martha's acceptance comes when she realizes her brother will spend all eternity with God (see v. 27). Mary's acceptance comes when she sees Jesus weep (v. 35). Whenever someone journeys with us in our pain, feeling it as deeply as we do, the healing process begins. When that compassion comes directly from God, the healing is accelerated tenfold.

Neither Martha nor Mary wants their "new normal" to be life without their brother. But when each accepts the comfort Jesus provides, they come to terms with that reality. It's then that the stone of each sister's cave is rolled back, revealing her heart and mind at peace. It's as if Jesus waits for God to resurrect the souls of Martha and Mary (the Bonus Miracle) before he raises the body of their brother. It shouldn't come as a surprise: God always prioritizes the healing of the soul over that of the body.

> *God always prioritizes the healing of the soul over that of the body.*

We have to believe that God is always ready and willing to heal our souls. That healing only happens, though, when we accept what cannot be and put our trust in him. As in any relationship, trust is built over time. Each time we extend trust to another person, and that person comes through for us, we trust him or her with a little bit more. It's no different with God. When we look back and identify all the ways God has been there for us, we naturally trust him with more. That's why it's important to recount the ways. We need to reflect back and revisit all the times we encountered hardships. When we spend time remembering how they were resolved, we're able to identify God's hand in their resolution.

To make the process more concrete, it's helpful to make a Faithfulness Board. Whether we use a bulletin board, a dry-erase board, or the Notes section on our phones, we can place images, objects, or words on them that capture all the times and ways God intervened on our behalf. The more visible our Faithfulness Board is, the more often we will see God's constant and steady support. The more we remember how he showed up for us in the past, the more willing we'll be to place our trust in him in the future.

A New Level of Trust

I've had several miscarriages in my vocation as a mother. Each one took a piece of my heart and left me fearful and anxious with every pregnancy thereafter. Somewhere along the line, my OB/GYN discovered I'm Rh negative. If a woman is Rh negative and her baby is Rh positive, her body creates antibodies that go after the baby in utero. It shocked me that my womb, the place that was supposed to be safe to grow and nurture a child, could actually choke out new life.

We didn't know if my being Rh negative was the reason for my previous miscarriages, but the new diagnosis clearly told me I had to approach any new pregnancy differently. Despite not wanting to be dependent on medication of any kind, my "new normal" from that point forward was accepting the solution provided: getting an injection of Rh immune globulin (RhIG) at twenty-eight weeks of any pregnancy and immediately after any delivery or loss. It's one thing to get that shot while holding a beautiful baby in your arms. It's a completely different story to get that shot when your womb and arms are left empty. Nothing humbled me more than realizing just how little control I had over life and the sustaining of it.

Eventually, I stopped getting pregnant altogether. My husband and I had to accept that our future had no more babies in it. We had two rambunctious boys who were the center of our world and filled our hearts to the brim. After counting ourselves fortunate for them, we gave away all our baby gear and turned our focus to raising our boys to be loving, kind, faith-filled people.

Imagine our surprise when, four years later, we discovered I was pregnant! We felt that crazy mixture of trepidation over what might not be, and sheer elation over what might. That elation tripled when the ultrasound tech said we were having a girl! Sadly, I had to immediately tamp down my excitement for fear of having further to fall if we lost her. That entire pregnancy became an exercise in putting my trust in God, believing he would carry me through if she wasn't meant to be and thanking him in advance if she was his will for us.

My daughter, Jocelyn, is one of the greatest reminders on my Faithfulness Board of just how extravagant God's love is. She is a complete gift, in every sense of the word, and I'm grateful for her every single day. But I'm also grateful for those nine and a half months that felt like time in a dark cave. While I waited for God's decision about her life, mine was changed. I learned and lived a whole new level of trust and acceptance that healed my soul, well before my daughter was born.

• •

At His Feet

Ever Faithful Redeemer,

Life can be hard, and I tend to resist that reality with every hardship I face. Prompt me to take whatever steps I can to address the circumstances. When a situation cannot be changed, help me to accept it with grace, knowing you are with me through it all. Open my heart and mind so I may feel you beside me in my pain. Help me to lean into you and allow your mighty hand to touch and heal my soul.

No matter how dark my cave, or how long I'm in it, give me the confidence to trust that you are working for my good. Transform me through the process, so when you do roll back the stone, I will step out into the light, reshaped by your mercy and grace.

Thank you for always showing up for me. Keep me ever mindful of all the ways you have resurrected me in the past. Deepen my trust in you each time I recall your extravagant love for me.

I ask this in Jesus' name. Amen.

Unwrapping the G-I-F-T

Gauge — Is there a difficulty I'm facing right now? How do I feel when I realize I may not be able to change the situation?

Invite — What happens when I invite those feelings in and sit with them at God's feet?

Filter — What do I see when I look at the situation through the filter of God's loving eyes?

Transform — What concrete steps can I take to accept whatever unresolvable situation I'm facing? How do I go about letting God reshape me through the process?

14
Surrendering at His Feet

*Six days before the Passover Jesus came to Bethany, the
home of Lazarus, whom he had raised from the dead.
There they gave a dinner for him. Martha served, and
Lazarus was one of those at the table with him. Mary
took a pound of costly perfume made of pure nard,
anointed Jesus' feet, and wiped them with her hair. The
house was filled with the fragrance of the perfume.*
— John 12:1–3

We've all seen images of Third World women carrying jugs
of water on their heads. It took living in Guatemala for me
to learn that they don't limit themselves to water. The women carry just about anything on their heads, be it a bin full of wet clothes
just washed at the river, firewood, a chair, even a chicken. No mat-

ter how heavy or awkward the item, they carry it, and themselves, with grace: their posture straight, their eyes focused straight ahead. Upon closer inspection, it became clear to me that as they move, everything aligns with their core. They use their center of gravity for both balance and strength.

Guatemalan men, however, wouldn't be caught dead carrying anything on top of their heads. They use their forehead. They wrap a rope around whatever they're transporting, attach a leather strap to it, crouch as low as the item, and put the leather strap across their brow. Then they stand and bend forward, distributing the weight of the item across their back and forehead. If it's something heavy, like a bureau, they might also need to use their neck and shoulder muscles while bent over in that stance. Unfortunately, this approach takes a toll over time. The younger men may still move about with ease, but the older men have become permanently stooped. Even when they have nothing to transport, their posture is hunched over, their eyes cast downward.

Bending Under the Burden

In John 12, posture isn't the only way Martha and Mary differ from each other. Per their usual, their behavior is different too. Martha is upright, busy with serving. Mary is prostrate, pouring perfume on Jesus' feet and wiping them with her hair. Where the sisters mirror each other is where they now draw their strength: from their core. At the very center of their being is a love for Jesus so deep, it inspired each of them to work through whatever had them off-balance and weak at the dinner party in Luke 10.

The old Martha was bent under the weight of serving when left to do it all alone. She viewed everything with her head — not the crown of it, but the front of it, where the frontal lobe is: the place in the brain that controls emotional expression, language, judgment, and problem-solving. The more her resentment grew, the heavier the weight strapped across her forehead became, skewing her judgment, hunching her over with her perceived burden, forcing her to look down. She exemplified that we always lose sight of our purpose when we stop looking up.

Like the greatest chiropractor ever, Jesus realigned Martha when she went to him. She surrendered her head-heavy posture, and he crowned her with one that was heart and core strong. Consequently, she now serves, in John 12, from the very center of her being, the place where every action, every gesture comes from love. She keeps her eyes focused straight ahead, no longer looking at others, no longer comparing herself and her actions to them, no longer keeping score. She now knows that serving matters. Jesus himself came to do it (see Lk 22:27). Having completely and irrevocably aligned her serving with her love for Jesus, there's no further mention of her in the Bible. There doesn't have to be. She has found her happily ever after: living out her purpose of providing for others while carrying herself upright with dignity, embodying "the better part" God predestined for her.

> *We always lose sight of our purpose when we stop looking up.*

As for Mary, the old her was passive and in need of her own realignment. As Edward Sri talks about in his book *Into His Likeness: Be Transformed as a Disciple of Christ*, Mary was more of a fan than a follower.* As if vying for the best seat at a rock concert, she liked being in the front row. Once there, though, she listened and wept. But as her relationship with Jesus grew, she learned to adopt a more active posture. She now takes action to be Jesus' hands and feet on earth, so much so that she pours perfume all

---

*Edward Sri, *Into His Likeness: Be Transformed as a Disciple of Christ* (San Francisco, CA, and Greenwood Village, CO: Ignatius Press and Augustine Institute, 2017), 13.

over his in her outpouring of devotion. She doesn't think about the cost or second-guess her actions. Her conviction comes from her core, the center of her soul, where there is no wavering. Being all in as a follower of Christ is her purpose in life now, and she lives it with the same spiritual posture of love and dignity that Martha does.

Our posture says a lot about us and how we view our lives. If we say one thing but feel another, our body language and how we carry ourselves will always give us away, if not in the short term, most assuredly in the long term. Over time, the misalignment pulls us off-balance and steers us toward tension. Stress, unchecked, always increases in weight, and the more we draw our strength from the wrong place, the more prone we are to label our struggle a "burden." Whether our burden is real or perceived, when we bend under it, we feel the repercussions of doing so. Inwardly, we feel an angst in our gut because our heart is out of harmony with our head. Outwardly, our posture shifts, pulling certain muscles in ways they shouldn't go as our body tries to compensate for the misalignment. That's not how God wants us to live. That's why he sent us his only-begotten Son, to show us how to carry ourselves and our struggles.

Surrendering at His Feet

If anyone had a right to bend under his burden, it was Jesus. He was asked to shoulder the sins of the world and nail them to the cross with his very own body. He may have fallen physically under the weight of the wooden beam on the road to Calvary, but never once did he bend spiritually. Rather, he yoked himself to his Father with complete and utter trust at all times. That trust was reflected in his upright posture in the wilderness when, famished from forty days of fasting, Satan tried to bend him with temptation (see Mt 4:1–11). He demonstrated his trust with his reclined and peacefully sleeping body in the back of a boat, despite a raging storm that tossed the boat about (Mk 4:35–41). He embodied his trust when God showed him the cup of his passion in the Garden of Gethsemane. The only thing that bent then were Jesus' knees, in prayer, as he first asked that the cup be taken away, and then in surrender when he fully accepted his Father's will. Luke 22:42–43 says: "'Father, if you are willing, remove this cup from me; yet, not my will but yours be done.' Then an angel from heaven appeared to him and gave him strength." This clarifies that it was *after* Jesus surrendered his will to his Father's that the Father sent Jesus an angel to give him strength. That's how it works for us too: When we surrender our will to God, he sends us angels to carry us through, strengthening us for our purpose.

In the upside-down world of faith, surrender comes from a stance of strength. Unlike on the battlefield, where it may be equated with losing, surrender in faith is sacred. Each time we hand it all over to God, the source of our strength moves from our forehead to our core. We're no longer depending on logic and reasoning to get us through. We're drawing strength from that place where

In the upside-down world of faith, surrender comes from a stance of strength.

God resides. It takes trust, for sure. But wisdom shows us that a lack of trust expands our burden, adding weight to it, like a dry sponge soaking up water. A faith-filled trust does the exact opposite. It reduces our burden like a vacuum to one of those space-saving bags, sucking out all the air and shrinking it in size. Additionally, the more we surrender to God, the more we see he's working for our good, not just despite our struggles, but in and through them.

When we do finally surrender with trust, we feel the weight of our burden shift from our shoulders to his, sometimes subtly, oftentimes profoundly. Suddenly, we can stand upright again and carry ourselves with dignity and grace. Like Jesus, the only bending we do at this stage is in prayer, as we praise and thank God for bringing us through.

On this side of heaven, we all have things that don't go our way. Some things even threaten to break us. When we have our mighty God standing at the ready to help — as he always is — all we need to do is take the necessary steps to surrender it all at his Son's feet. To do so, we must first define the real struggle — not the symptoms but the origin of the problem itself. Then we can determine how we're carrying it. Are we drawing strength from our forehead (the place of reason and logic) as we try to shoulder it alone? Or are we drawing strength from our core, yoking ourselves to God for help?

The best way to know is to assess how we're feeling. It's not uncommon for our spiritual struggles to manifest themselves in physical ways. Inwardly, do we have that sensation of angst or tension in our gut? Outwardly, do we feel a tightness in any of our muscles, telling us they're being pulled in ways they shouldn't be? If so, our bodies could be telling us we're carrying it all wrong, drawing our strength from ourselves rather than from God. This is where meditation and visualization can be very helpful. Focusing on the place in our bodies where we store our stress, we then visualize removing that tension and handing it over to God.

Next, we imagine him taking it from us, filling that now empty space with his grace and love. The more clearly we can picture it, like watching a movie, the more successful the exercise. We know we're doing it right when we feel a physical or spiritual change for the better. Whether we meditate and visualize in short increments (while driving in our car, brushing our teeth, and so forth) or take longer stretches of time in a quiet room, the more we practice surrendering to him, the more we'll feel a distinct difference in our body, and in our soul.

The Ergonomics of Surrender

When our washing machine broke a few years back, I bought a new one online at Best Buy. A few days later, two guys showed up to deliver and install it. These guys weren't your typical movers. In fact, they didn't look very strong at all. I felt terrible telling them the laundry room was on the second floor. Despite their lack of muscle, however, they didn't blink an eye. Each one strapped on a leather harness that looked like a cross between a weight belt and German lederhosen, with a long strap and hook that hung down to their knees. I watched in amazement as they bent their knees, attached their hooks to the bottom of the washer, and then stood up. Like magic, the machine seemed to float in the air, as they stood perfectly straight. Almost effortlessly, they carried that two-hundred-pound washing machine up my flight of stairs without ever bending over. It was the greatest example of ergonomics replacing brawn I've ever seen.

God has fashioned one of those fancy harnesses for each one of us. Whether our struggle feels like two hundred pounds or two thousand, when we surrender it to him, he lifts up our burden and us. We may still have to carry a portion of the load, but we'll do so with our back straight and our head and heart held high. As we move forward, we'll exude the grace he strengthens us with, always.

• •

At His Feet

Great Burden Bearer,

When I'm faced with a task or difficult situation I'd prefer to avoid, remind me that I always get to choose my attitude and approach. If I choose wrong, stress will add weight to my struggle, pulling me down and off-balance. Align my head and my heart so I'll choose the better part, carrying things out in your Son's name. Nothing may change on the outside, but everything will change inside of me, turning my initial sacrifice into an opportunity to bless others with your mercy and love.

When a truly heavy struggle comes my way, keep me from bending under my burden. Remind me that a bent-over posture inevitably results in problems you never intended for me. Gently lead me to your Son's feet, where I can surrender my head-heavy posture and be crowned with one that's heart and core strong. Keep me mindful that when I do finally surrender my will to you, you'll send angels to strengthen me. Once yoked to you, I'll carry my portion of the weight, drawing from your strength, not my own. That's how I'll hold my head and heart high so my sight can remain on you.

I ask this in Jesus' name. Amen.

———————————

Unwrapping the G-I-F-T

Gauge — Are there any burdens I'm bending under right now? How does that make me feel — physically, mentally, and spiritually?

Invite — What happens when I invite those feelings in and sit with them at God's feet?

Filter —What do I see when I look at the situation through the filter of God's loving eyes?

Transform — What concrete steps can I take to surrender my burdens to God?

Conclusion

*But Judas Iscariot, one of the disciples (the one who
was about to betray him), said, "Why was this perfume
not sold for three hundred denarii and the money
given to the poor?" (He said this not because he cared
about the poor, but because he was a thief; he kept the
common purse and used to steal what was put into it.)
Jesus said, "Leave her alone. She bought it so that she
might keep it for the day of my burial. You always have
the poor with you, but you do not always have me."*
— John 12:4–8

In place of a scrapbook, I have a memory box filled with items
from my mission years in Guatemala. If you looked inside,
you'd see photos, airline tickets, letters and drawings from my
students, and other miscellaneous items. Each would seem to

have just one dimension. But when *I* look inside that box, those items have more dimensions than I can count. They're portals back in time, instantly reminding me of rich experiences filled with people, landscapes, smells, tastes, and sounds. They capture the essence of marvelous adventures and heartbreaking ordeals. Tough times included, I wouldn't change a thing. My experiences there transformed my life and my relationship with God, all in tremendous ways.

As we journeyed through this book, we witnessed Martha and Mary transform in tremendous ways too. In the midst of experiencing all three levels of tension, both sisters knew to go to Jesus for help to resolve the tension. They recognized that the source of tension never begins with God, but he'll always be its end if we bring it to him. At the dinner party, Martha and Mary's individual experiences became a portal for us to look through and learn that if we respond to God's gentle nudge, we diffuse tension at its lowest level. If, however, we grab the rope of tension and pull it tight, refusing to make a change, tension escalates into the mid-level zone. That's when an *outward* change is required to transform our tension into grace.

> *The source of tension never begins with God, but he'll always be its end if we bring it to him.*

When their brother, Lazarus, died, the sisters showed us that going to God with our high-level tension gives us the opportunity to reclaim our choice and make an *inward* change. When we do so, not only does tension turn into grace, but we also become blessed with Bonus Miracles abounding with peace and joy.

The sisters are two multidimensional examples of how the

G-I-F-T process works, so much so that their transformations are recorded in the Bible for all eternity. That's how we see the introverted Mary of Luke 10 become the extravagant follower in John 12, pouring expensive oil on Jesus' feet. That's how we see the score-keeping Martha of Luke 10 become so extraordinary in her serving in John 12, Mary's behavior no longer fills her with tension. (It fills Judas with tension, but that's an entirely different story.)

My hope is that after you read this book, it will become a memory box for you, filled with reminders to turn to God in your tension. He doesn't care about the motive for our visit. He's just thrilled we show up at his door. Like an artist who can create beauty using just about anything, God can create grace from whatever we bring to him, tension included. He uses it to weave a cord that gently draws us closer to him so he can show us the gift our tension holds. When we apply that gift to our lives, it becomes its own portal, transporting us to the peace and joy God wants to bless us with always.

ACKNOWLEDGMENTS

It's a dream come true to finally write and publish a book. It's also a dream come true to publicly acknowledge and thank all of the people who got me to this point.

To Deborah Shelby, the first person to welcome me into the blogging world back in 2014, thank you for being a faithful reader and wonderful friend ever since. To Fr. Brian Kennedy and all the staff and parishioners of St. Matthew Church, thank you for embracing every one of my MOSAIC of Faith ministries. To Sr. Margretta Flanagan, please accept my deepest gratitude for the twenty-plus years of spiritual direction that have led me closer to God. To Br. Paul O'Keeffe, your feedback, support, and networking on my behalf is greatly appreciated. To Fr. Daniel P. Horan, thank you for imparting your wisdom about how to get published. To Sr. Bridget Haase, sharing your connections and teaching me to start each writing day in prayer have transformed my career. To all the people in the Christian publishing world I've crossed paths with — Terence Hegarty, Pat Gohn, Kandi Zeller, Pastor Mary Lindberg, Jessica Miller Kelley, Janet Talbert, and Becky McDaniel — your acceptance of and belief in my work inspired me to reach further.

I'm immensely grateful to Lisa Hendey for allowing me to join the CatholicMom.com writing community; Danielle Bean, for graciously agreeing to write my foreword; and Barb Szyszkiewicz, for lifting me up professionally and personally. I've been blessed beyond measure by Sarah Reinhard who saw potential in the pitch I made for this book back in 2018; Kelly Guest, my fellow OSV author who journeyed with me through this process; Mary Beth (Baker) Giltner, whose insight and expertise took my proposal and manuscript to an entirely new level, resulting in the book you now hold in your hands; Rebecca (Willen) Martin, who gracefully carried my manuscript over the finish line; and Neal Quandt, who went the distance with his stellar finishing touch. To Gina Brannon, of Sweet Love Studios, thank you for the time and talent you devoted to producing my headshot for the back cover.

To all the women of MOSAIC of Faith, your involvement in and encouragement of my ministries is appreciated more than you'll ever know. To Jess Weller and Pam Sarantis, two of the greatest friends a person could ask for, you are my heroes for taking my kids so I could write, building my first website and social media accounts (because this tech-challenged girl couldn't have done it herself), cheering me on from the very beginning, and carrying me through it all. To my sisters, Colleen Marek, Elaine Ferguson, and Kerry Duprez, every word in this book (especially chapter 3!) was made better by your love and prayers. To my mom, Helen Dignan, who calls herself my "Biggest Fan," being your daughter is the greatest blessing of my life! Words cannot express the depth of my gratitude for your ever-constant love and support for every single thing I have ever done.

To my kids, Zack, Mason, and Jocelyn, thank you for being just as excited about each step in this journey as I've been. With your hooting and cheering, being my first follower on Twitter (Zack), building LEGO creations to inspire me (Mason), and leaving love notes on my computer (Jocelyn), you've made this a team effort and a complete joy. To my husband, John, your unwavering support, through both words and actions, has been incredible. Whether it's cooking meals, entertaining our kids, or doing some of my chores to give me more time to write; reading multiple chapters to give me feedback; or doubling your efforts at work to carry us through, I could not have done this without you.

Above all, to God, thank you for choosing me to write this book and for partnering with me every step of the way. May it get into as many hands as possible to draw more people to you.

About the Author

Claire McGarry is the author of the Lenten family devotionals *With Our Savior* and *Abundant Mercy*, published by Creative Communications for the Family and Bayard, Inc. Her freelance work has appeared in multiple *Chicken Soup for the Soul* books and various magazines and devotionals. The founder of MOSAIC of Faith, a ministry with several programs for mothers and children, she contributes to *Living Faith*, *Mornings with Jesus,* CatholicMom, and blogs at *Shifting My Perspective*. She lives in New Hampshire with her husband and three children.

P.S. I would love to hear how this book has impacted you. Please feel free to leave a comment on my Facebook Author Page or on my website www.clairemcgarry.com. I look forward to hearing from you!

You might also like:

Draw Close to Jesus:
A Woman's Guide to Eucharistic Adoration
By Merridith Frediani

Jesus counted many women among his closest followers during his earthly ministry. He encountered, forgave, and healed women, and their lives were changed forever.

Our lives are also changed when we spend time with Jesus in Eucharistic adoration. **Draw Close to Jesus: A Woman's Guide to Eucharistic Adoration** offers women heartfelt, practical guidance for meeting Jesus in adoration and allowing him to transform us.

> "In this beautiful work, Merridith Frediani provides women with all the means needed to pursue holiness! The book's use of Scripture is endearing and uplifting, making the Lord's presence more richly felt and experienced by those in Adoration. Draw Close to Jesus: A Woman's Guide to Eucharistic Adoration takes the feminine genius to a whole new level in the spiritual life."
> — Father Jeffrey Kirby, STD, author of Way of the Cross for Loved Ones Who Have Left the Faith

Available at
OSVCatholicBookstore.com
or wherever books are sold